Java Programming for Beginners *Learn Java from the Ground Up*

A Step-by-Step Guide to Writing Java Applications and Programs

MIGUEL FARMER

RAFAEL SANDER

All rights reserved

Table of Content

TABLE OF CONTENTS

INTRODUCTION 7

Java Programming for Beginners: Learn Java from the
Ground Up 7

   Conclusion 13

Chapter 1 14

Introduction to Java Programming...............................14

   Conclusion 23

Chapter 2 25

Understanding Java Syntax 25

   Conclusion 36

Chapter 3 37

Java Data Types and Variables 37

   Conclusion 49

Chapter 4 50

Control Flow Statements: Conditionals and Loops 50

   Conclusion 62

Chapter 5 63

Arrays and Collections in Java.....................................63

   Conclusion 74

Chapter 6 76

Methods in Java 76

   Conclusion 86

Chapter 7 88

Object-Oriented Programming (OOP) Concepts 88

Conclusion 103

Chapter 8 104

Classes and Objects in Java 104

Conclusion 115

Chapter 9 117

Inheritance and Interfaces 117

Conclusion 129

Chapter 10 130

Exception Handling in Java 130

Conclusion 141

Chapter 11 143

Java Collections Framework 143

Conclusion 156

Chapter 12 158

Java Streams and Lambda Expressions 158

Conclusion 169

Chapter 13 170

File Handling in Java 170

Conclusion 181

Chapter 14 182

Java GUI Programming: Swing and JavaFX 182

Conclusion 195

Chapter 15 196

Working with Databases in Java 196

Conclusion 212

Chapter 16 213

Multithreading and Concurrency 213

    Conclusion 226

Chapter 17 228

Networking in Java 228

    Conclusion 239

Chapter 18 241

Working with JSON and XML in Java 241

    Conclusion 256

Chapter 19 258

Java Reflection and Annotations 258

    Conclusion 270

Chapter 20 272

Unit Testing with JUnit 272

    Conclusion 285

Chapter 21 286

Java Security 286

    Conclusion 299

Chapter 22 301

Design Patterns in Java 301

Chapter 23 310

Java 8 and Beyond: New Features 310

Chapter 24 322

Java Virtual Machine (JVM) and Memory Management 322

    Conclusion 331

Chapter 25 333

Building Web Applications with Java 333

Chapter 26 346

Advanced Java Topics 346

Chapter 27...359

Best Practices and Final Thoughts 359

INTRODUCTION

Java Programming for Beginners: Learn Java from the Ground Up

Welcome to **"Java Programming for Beginners: Learn Java from the Ground Up"**! Whether you're just starting your programming journey or looking to deepen your understanding of Java, this book is designed to guide you every step of the way. From the fundamentals to advanced topics, we'll cover everything you need to build a solid foundation and gain the skills necessary to develop powerful, real-world Java applications.

Java is one of the most widely used programming languages in the world. Its versatility, portability, and scalability make it an ideal choice for developing applications ranging from mobile apps and web applications to large-scale enterprise systems. By learning Java, you unlock a world of opportunities in software development, backed by a vast ecosystem of libraries, frameworks, and tools.

This book is specifically crafted to help both **beginners** and those with some programming experience understand Java's core concepts, syntax, and best practices. We will approach learning Java in a structured, easy-to-follow manner, with a focus on **real-world examples** to demonstrate the concepts you will encounter. Whether you're a complete novice or someone looking to refresh your skills, the approach used in this book ensures a smooth learning curve.

Why Learn Java?

Java has been the backbone of enterprise-level applications for decades. Some key reasons why Java is still the go-to language for developers include:

Platform Independence: Java's famous slogan, "Write once, run anywhere," means that Java applications can run on any platform that supports the Java Virtual Machine (JVM). This is a key feature that allows developers to build applications for desktops, servers, and mobile devices without worrying about compatibility issues.

Rich Ecosystem: The Java ecosystem is vast. With frameworks like **Spring**, **Hibernate**, and **JavaFX**, as well as tools like **Maven**, **Gradle**, and **JUnit**, Java developers have everything they need to build, test, and deploy applications efficiently.

Strong Community Support: Java has a long history and a large, active community of developers who contribute to open-source projects, create tutorials, and build libraries that simplify development.

Enterprise-Grade Solutions: Many of the world's largest companies use Java for their backend systems. Its stability, scalability, and security features make it a top choice for enterprise applications.

How This Book is Structured

This book is divided into **27 chapters**, each focusing on a different aspect of Java programming, from basic syntax to more advanced concepts like **concurrency**, **JVM tuning**, and **design patterns**. Each chapter is carefully crafted to be:

Clear and **Concise**: No complex jargon or unnecessary theory. Every concept is explained simply and clearly, with practical examples.

Hands-On: You'll learn Java by doing. Every concept is reinforced with **real-world examples** and **exercises** to give you immediate, practical experience.

Progressive: The chapters are arranged logically to help you build your knowledge step by step. We'll start with basic concepts like **variables and data types** and gradually move toward complex topics like **memory management** and **Java performance optimization**.

What You Will Learn

Java Syntax and Basic Concepts: We'll begin with the essentials like variables, data types, loops, and conditionals. You'll learn how to write your first Java programs and understand the building blocks of Java syntax.

Object-Oriented Programming (OOP): Java is an **object-oriented language**, and understanding concepts like **classes**, **objects**, **inheritance**, **polymorphism**, and **encapsulation** is crucial for building real-world applications.

Advanced Topics: As you progress, we'll introduce more advanced topics like **concurrency**, **parallelism**, and **memory management**, ensuring you're ready to tackle performance-sensitive and large-scale applications.

Web Development: You'll also learn how to build **web applications** using **Java servlets, JSP**, and **RESTful APIs**. We will cover frameworks like **Spring** to give you the tools needed for modern enterprise development.

Best Practices and Optimization: Finally, we'll show you how to write **clean, maintainable code**, adhere to **coding standards**, and optimize your code for better performance, helping you become a well-rounded Java developer.

Why This Book is Different

Unlike many programming books that focus on theory or abstract examples, this book emphasizes practical, **real-world programming**. Every concept is supported by examples and projects that demonstrate how Java is used in industry-standard applications. You'll also find several **hands-on exercises** and **code challenges** designed to deepen your understanding and help you apply what you've learned.

Additionally, this book not only focuses on learning Java but also encourages you to think like a software engineer, with **best practices** for writing **clean code**, improving performance, and managing complexity. The end goal isn't just to learn Java, but to **become a proficient Java developer** who can build robust, scalable, and maintainable software.

Who This Book Is For

Beginners: If you are new to programming, this book is perfect for you. It starts with the very basics, teaching you how to think like a programmer and guiding you step-by-step through the learning process.

Experienced Programmers: If you are familiar with programming in other languages, this book will help you learn Java's syntax and paradigms, with a focus on Java-specific features like memory management and concurrency.

Developers Looking to Level Up: If you are already writing Java but want to deepen your understanding, this book covers advanced topics such as JVM tuning, threading, and performance optimization, ensuring you're ready for real-world, production-level Java development.

How to Use This Book

Follow Along: Read the chapters in order to build a solid understanding of each concept. The examples and exercises are designed to reinforce what you've learned.

Practice: Complete the exercises and real-world projects to apply what you've learned. The more you practice, the better you'll understand Java.

Refactor and Improve: Go back to your old projects and refactor them as you learn new techniques. Try applying the best practices and modern Java features to your existing code.

Conclusion

Java is a powerful, versatile language that has stood the test of time. With the skills you'll gain from this book, you will not only be able to write Java applications but also build a strong foundation for tackling complex software development challenges.

By the end of this book, you will have the skills needed to develop a wide range of applications, from **simple console programs** to **large-scale enterprise systems**. You'll also gain an understanding of the best practices, design principles, and tools used by professional developers to ensure code is efficient, maintainable, and scalable.

Let's get started on your Java development journey!

CHAPTER 1

INTRODUCTION TO JAVA PROGRAMMING

Overview of Java

Java is one of the most widely used programming languages today. Originally developed by **James Gosling** and his team at **Sun Microsystems** in 1991, Java is an object-oriented, platform-independent language designed to be **simple**, **secure**, and **robust**. It was created with the goal of allowing developers to write software that could run on any platform without modification, a principle known as **Write Once, Run Anywhere (WORA)**.

Java is used in a variety of domains, including:

Web Development: Java is widely used to build server-side applications using frameworks like **Spring** and **Java EE**.

Enterprise Applications: It powers many enterprise-level applications due to its scalability and performance.

Mobile Development: Java was the primary language for building Android applications, although Kotlin is also now commonly used.

Big Data: Java is used in data processing frameworks like **Hadoop** and **Apache Spark**.

Embedded Systems: Java is also used in embedded systems and IoT devices.

Java's versatility, reliability, and large developer community make it a go-to language for developers worldwide.

History and Evolution of Java

Java was first created as a part of the **Green Project** at **Sun Microsystems**. The original idea was to build software for **consumer electronics**, such as set-top boxes. However, over time, Java evolved into a general-purpose programming language.

Key milestones in Java's evolution:

1995: Java was officially released by Sun Microsystems. It was designed as a portable, platform-independent language that could run on any device with a Java Virtual Machine (JVM).

1996: The first official version of Java (Java 1.0) was released.

2004: Sun Microsystems released **Java 5**, which introduced major features like **generics, metadata annotations**, and **enhanced for-loops**.

2006: Sun released Java as an open-source language.

2009: Oracle Corporation acquired **Sun Microsystems** and, thus, took over the stewardship of Java.

2017: **Java 9** introduced the **module system**, and **Java 10** introduced local-variable type inference (the `var` keyword).

2021: **Java 16** and later versions continue to improve the performance, security, and modularity of the language, along with regular feature updates.

Why Learn Java?

Java is a popular choice for developers and has a wide range of applications. Here are some reasons why learning Java is valuable:

Platform Independence: Java's **WORA** principle allows developers to write code once and run it on any device that supports Java. This is made possible by the **Java Virtual Machine (JVM)**, which allows Java programs to run on different operating systems such as **Windows**, **Mac**, and **Linux**.

Strong Community and Resources: Java has one of the largest communities of developers, meaning that help is always readily available. Countless tutorials, documentation, and forums make it easy for new developers to get started.

Mature Ecosystem: Java has a **mature ecosystem** of libraries, tools, and frameworks. Whether you are building **web applications**, **enterprise systems**, or working with **big data**, Java has a library or framework to support your needs.

Performance and Scalability: Java is known for its **high performance** and scalability. It can handle large-scale applications, making it a preferred choice for enterprise-level systems.

Career Opportunities: Java remains one of the most in-demand programming languages in the job market, particularly in sectors like **financial services, enterprise software, mobile development**, and **cloud computing**.

Java Programming for Beginners

Installing Java Development Kit (JDK) and Setting Up an IDE

Before you start programming in Java, you need to install the **Java Development Kit (JDK)** and set up an **Integrated Development Environment (IDE)**. The JDK includes everything needed to develop Java applications, including the **Java Runtime Environment (JRE)**, the Java compiler, and tools for debugging and monitoring Java applications.

Step 1: Download and Install JDK

- Visit the official Oracle website and download the latest version of the **JDK** for your operating system (Windows, macOS, or Linux).

- Follow the installation instructions to install the JDK on your machine.

- After installing the JDK, set the **PATH** variable on your system to include the JDK's **bin** directory, so you can run Java commands from the terminal or command prompt.

Step 2: Set Up an IDE

While you can write Java programs in any text editor, it's highly recommended to use an **IDE** for better productivity. **Eclipse** and **IntelliJ IDEA** are two popular Java IDEs, both offering features

18

such as syntax highlighting, code completion, debugging tools, and project management.

Installing Eclipse:

Download Eclipse from the official website.

Follow the installation instructions for your operating system.

Open Eclipse, and configure the workspace where you'll save your Java projects.

Installing IntelliJ IDEA:

Download IntelliJ IDEA from the official website.

Install and configure the IDE.

Open IntelliJ, create a new Java project, and select the JDK installed earlier.

Once your IDE is set up, you can start writing Java programs and running them directly within the IDE.

Writing Your First Java Program: "Hello, World!"

The classic **"Hello, World!"** program is the first program that every Java developer writes. It serves as a simple introduction to Java syntax and helps verify that everything is set up correctly.

Here's how you can write and run your first Java program in your IDE:

Create a New Java Project: In your IDE, create a new Java project and name it something like "HelloWorld".

Create a Java Class: Inside the project, create a new Java class called `HelloWorld`. Every Java application must contain a class, and the class name should match the filename (i.e., `HelloWorld.java`).

Write the Program: In the `HelloWorld` class, add the following code:

```java
public class HelloWorld {
    public static void main(String[] args) {
        System.out.println("Hello, World!");  // Print greeting to the console
    }
}
```

Explanation of the Code:

`public class HelloWorld`: This defines a class named `HelloWorld`. The `public` keyword means that the class is accessible from anywhere.

`public static void main(String[] args)`: This is the **main method**, which is the entry point for any Java program. When you run the program, the code inside the `main` method is executed.

`System.out.println("Hello, World!");`: This prints the string "Hello, World!" to the console. `System.out` refers to the standard output stream, and `println` prints a message followed by a newline.

Run the Program: After writing the code, you can run the program directly within the IDE. The output should be:

```
Hello, World!
```

Congratulations! You've just written your first Java program. This simple program introduces some of the core concepts of Java programming, such as classes, methods, and output to the console.

Real-World Example: Creating a Simple Console Application to Greet the User

Now that you've written your first "Hello, World!" program, let's extend it into a more interactive program by asking the user for their name and then greeting them.

Here's how you can modify your program:

```java
import java.util.Scanner;  // Import Scanner class to take input from the user

public class GreetUser {
    public static void main(String[] args) {
        Scanner scanner = new Scanner(System.in);  // Create a Scanner object to read input

        System.out.print("Enter your name: ");  // Prompt user for their name
        String name = scanner.nextLine();  // Read the input from the user

        System.out.println("Hello, " + name + "!");  // Greet the user
    }
}
```

22

Explanation of the Code:

`import java.util.Scanner;`: This imports the `Scanner` class, which is used to read user input from the console.

`Scanner scanner = new Scanner(System.in);`: This creates a `Scanner` object that listens for user input from the standard input stream (`System.in`).

`String name = scanner.nextLine();`: This reads a line of text input from the user and stores it in the `name` variable.

`System.out.println("Hello, " + name + "!");`: This prints a personalized greeting using the name the user entered.

Conclusion

In this chapter, we have covered the basics of Java programming, including:

The **history** and **evolution** of Java.

Why Java is a valuable language to learn.

Installing the JDK and setting up an IDE (Eclipse or IntelliJ IDEA).

Writing and running your first **"Hello, World!"** program.

Creating a **real-world application** to greet the user by asking for their name.

With this foundation in place, you're now ready to dive deeper into the features and capabilities of Java. The next chapters will build upon these basics, introducing more advanced concepts, data structures, and algorithms to help you become proficient in Java programming.

Let's continue the journey to becoming a Java expert!

CHAPTER 2

UNDERSTANDING JAVA SYNTAX

In this chapter, we will dive into the **syntax structure** of Java, which is the foundation of writing code in this language. A solid understanding of syntax is crucial because it dictates how we write and structure our Java programs. We'll explore how Java uses **variables**, **data types**, and **constants**, as well as various **operators** and how to format and comment code for clarity and readability.

Java's Syntax Structure

Java's syntax is heavily influenced by **C** and is designed to be **simple** and **consistent**. Java code consists of statements, expressions, and declarations, each with its own structure.

Key points to understand:

Statements: These are the building blocks of Java programs. A statement is an instruction that tells the program to do something. Most statements in Java end with a semicolon (*;*), such as variable declarations, method calls, and expressions.

Blocks: Blocks are enclosed by curly braces { } and contain one or more statements. For example, the body of a method, class, or loop is a block.

Whitespace: Java ignores extra spaces and new lines, meaning you can format code for readability by adding spaces or new lines wherever needed.

Here's a simple structure of a Java program:

```java
public class MyClass {  // Class declaration

    public static void main(String[] args) {  //
Method declaration (entry point)
        // Statements go here
    }
}
```

Variables, Data Types, and Constants

Variables are containers for storing data, and in Java, you must specify the type of data each variable holds. Java is a **statically typed** language, which means the type of every variable must be explicitly defined at compile time.

1. Variables

A **variable** is a named storage location that holds data that can change during program execution. To declare a variable, you must specify its **type** and **name**.

```java
int age;   // Declaration of an integer variable
age = 25; // Initialization of the variable with a value
```

2. Data Types

Java has two types of data types:

Primitive Data Types: These represent basic types of data and are built into the language. Examples include:

int: A 32-bit signed integer.

double: A double-precision floating-point number.

char: A single 16-bit Unicode character.

boolean: Represents true or false.

```java
int age = 25;
```

27

```
double price = 19.99;
char grade = 'A';
boolean isJavaFun = true;
```

Reference Data Types: These are used to store references to objects or arrays. A **String** is one of the most commonly used reference data types in Java.

java

```
String name = "John Doe";
```

3. Constants

In Java, constants are values that cannot be changed once they are set. You can define constants using the `final` keyword.

java

```
final int MAX_VALUE = 100;   // MAX_VALUE cannot
be modified later
```

Operators: Arithmetic, Logical, Relational

Operators are symbols used to perform operations on variables and values. Java supports several types of operators:

1. Arithmetic Operators

These operators are used to perform mathematical operations like addition, subtraction, multiplication, and division.

java

```java
int a = 10;
int b = 5;
int sum = a + b;   // Addition
int difference = a - b;   // Subtraction
int product = a * b;   // Multiplication
int quotient = a / b;   // Division
int remainder = a % b;   // Modulus (remainder)
```

2. Logical Operators

Logical operators are used to perform logical operations, usually with **boolean** values. They help in decision-making processes within the program.

AND (&&): Returns true if both conditions are true.

OR (||): Returns true if either condition is true.

NOT (!): Inverts the boolean value.

java

```java
boolean isAdult = true;
```

29

```
boolean hasPermission = false;

if (isAdult && hasPermission) {
    System.out.println("Access granted.");
} else {
    System.out.println("Access denied.");
}
```

3. Relational Operators

These operators are used to compare two values and return a boolean result (true or false).

Equal to (==): Checks if two values are equal.

Not equal to (!=): Checks if two values are not equal.

Greater than (>): Checks if the left value is greater than the right.

Less than (<): Checks if the left value is less than the right.

Greater than or equal to (>=): Checks if the left value is greater than or equal to the right.

Less than or equal to (<=): Checks if the left value is less than or equal to the right.

```
java
```

```
int x = 10;
int y = 20;

boolean result = x < y;   // true, because 10 is
less than 20
```

Comments and Java Code Formatting

Comments in Java are used to explain and clarify the code. Java supports three types of comments:

Single-line comment: Used for short explanations on a single line.

java

```
int a = 10;   // This is a single-line
comment
```

Multi-line comment: Used for longer explanations spanning multiple lines.

java

```
/*
 This is a multi-line comment
 which can span across multiple lines.
*/
```

Javadoc comment: Used to generate documentation for classes, methods, and fields. They start with /** and end with */.

```java

/**
 * This method calculates the sum of two
numbers.
 * @param a The first number.
 * @param b The second number.
 * @return The sum of a and b.
 */
public int sum(int a, int b) {
    return a + b;
}
```

Code Formatting Best Practices

Indentation: Proper indentation is crucial for readability. Use consistent spacing (usually four spaces per indent) and curly braces {} even for single-line blocks.

Naming Conventions: Use meaningful names for variables, classes, and methods. For example:

Variables: int age, String userName

Classes: class Employee

Methods: `public void calculateSalary()`

Real-World Example: Implementing a Basic Calculator Using Operators

Now that we've covered the fundamentals of Java syntax, let's put it into practice by creating a simple calculator that can perform basic arithmetic operations.

Calculator Program:
java

```java
import java.util.Scanner;    // Import Scanner class for user input

public class Calculator {
    public static void main(String[] args) {
        Scanner scanner = new Scanner(System.in);  // Create scanner object to read input

        System.out.print("Enter first number: ");
        double num1 = scanner.nextDouble();   // Read the first number

        System.out.print("Enter second number: ");
```

33

```java
        double num2 = scanner.nextDouble();   //
Read the second number

        System.out.print("Enter an operator (+,
-, *, /): ");
        char           operator           =
scanner.next().charAt(0);   // Read the operator

        double result = 0;   // Variable to store
the result

        // Perform calculation based on operator
        switch (operator) {
            case '+':
                result = num1 + num2;
                break;
            case '-':
                result = num1 - num2;
                break;
            case '*':
                result = num1 * num2;
                break;
            case '/':
                if (num2 != 0) {
                    result = num1 / num2;
                } else {
                    System.out.println("Error:
Division by zero.");
```

```
            return;   // Exit if division
by zero
        }
        break;
    default:
        System.out.println("Invalid
operator.");
        return;
    }

    System.out.println("Result: " + result);
// Print the result
    }
}
```

Explanation:

> **User Input**: We use Scanner to get input from the user for two numbers and an operator.

> **Switch-Case**: The switch-case statement checks which operator the user entered and performs the corresponding operation.

> **Error Handling**: The program handles division by zero to avoid errors.

Sample Output:

35

```
sql

Enter first number: 5
Enter second number: 3
Enter an operator (+, -, *, /): +
Result: 8.0
```

Conclusion

In this chapter, we've covered the essential building blocks of Java syntax:

Variables and **data types** that define the kind of data your program handles.

Operators to perform operations on data.

Comments and **formatting** to improve the readability and maintainability of your code.

Using these fundamentals, we built a **basic calculator** application that performs arithmetic operations. In the next chapter, we'll dive deeper into **control flow** statements, where you'll learn how to control the flow of your programs with **conditionals** and **loops**.

CHAPTER 3

JAVA DATA TYPES AND VARIABLES

In this chapter, we'll explore the foundation of data handling in Java, focusing on **data types** and **variables**. Understanding how to work with different types of data is essential for writing effective Java programs. We will cover both **primitive** and **non-primitive data types**, type **casting** and **conversion**, as well as the **scope** and **lifetime** of variables. By the end of this chapter, you will be equipped to use data types appropriately in your Java applications.

Primitive Data Types in Java

Java is a **statically typed** language, which means that every variable must be declared with a data type. **Primitive data types** represent the simplest form of data and are the building blocks of more complex data structures.

Java has eight primitive data types:

   byte: A 8-bit signed integer (range from -128 to 127).

short: A 16-bit signed integer (range from -32,768 to 32,767).

int: A 32-bit signed integer (range from -2^{31} to $2^{31}-1$).

long: A 64-bit signed integer (range from -2^{63} to $2^{63}-1$).

float: A single-precision 32-bit floating-point number.

double: A double-precision 64-bit floating-point number.

char: A 16-bit Unicode character, used to store characters.

boolean: Represents either `true` or `false`.

Examples of Primitive Data Types:
java

```java
byte byteValue = 120;
short shortValue = 15000;
int intValue = 50000;
long longValue = 100000L;      // 'L' suffix indicates long value
float floatValue = 3.14f;      // 'f' suffix indicates float value
double doubleValue = 3.14159265359;
char charValue = 'A';  // Single character
boolean booleanValue = true;  // True or false
```

Each of these types has specific memory requirements and ranges, which helps Java manage memory efficiently.

Non-Primitive Data Types in Java

Non-primitive data types are objects or references to objects. These types are more complex than primitive types and can hold multiple values or more detailed structures.

String: A sequence of characters. Strings in Java are immutable, meaning once a String object is created, it cannot be changed.

java

```
String greeting = "Hello, World!";
```

Arrays: An array is a collection of variables of the same type stored at contiguous memory locations. Arrays can hold **primitive** data types or **objects**.

java

```
int[] numbers = {1, 2, 3, 4, 5};
String[]    names    =    {"Alice",    "Bob",
"Charlie"};
```

Classes and Objects: A class is a blueprint for creating objects, and an object is an instance of a class. You define a class with properties (fields) and methods.

39

```java

class Person {
    String name;
    int age;

    void introduce() {
        System.out.println("Hello, my name
is " + name);
    }
}

// Create an object of the Person class
Person person1 = new Person();
person1.name = "Alice";
person1.age = 25;
person1.introduce();
```

Type Casting and Conversions

Type casting refers to converting one data type into another. In Java, type casting can happen in two ways:

Implicit Casting (Widening): This happens when a smaller data type is automatically converted to a larger one. It doesn't require explicit casting.

```java
```

```
int intValue = 10;
double doubleValue = intValue;  // int to
double (automatically done)
```

Explicit Casting (Narrowing): When converting a larger data type to a smaller one, explicit casting is required. This may result in loss of data.

```
java
```

```
double doubleValue = 9.99;
int intValue = (int) doubleValue;  //
Explicit cast required, decimal part lost
```

Type Conversion also occurs when converting between primitive types and objects, such as converting a **String** to an **int** or vice versa:

```
java
```

```
String str = "123";
int num = Integer.parseInt(str);  // Converting
String to int
String newStr = String.valueOf(num);  //
Converting int to String
```

41

Scope and Lifetime of Variables

The **scope** of a variable refers to where it is accessible within your program. The **lifetime** of a variable refers to how long the variable exists in memory.

1. Local Variables

> **Scope**: Local variables are defined inside a method or block and can only be accessed within that method or block.

> **Lifetime**: They exist only during the execution of the method or block where they are declared.

Example:

```java
java

public void calculateSum() {
    int sum = 0;   // Local variable
    sum = 5 + 10;
    System.out.println(sum);
}
// 'sum' is only accessible within the method
'calculateSum'
```

2. Instance Variables

Scope: Instance variables are declared inside a class but outside any method. They can be accessed by all methods in that class.

Lifetime: Instance variables exist as long as the object of the class is alive.

Example:

```java

class Car {
    String model;  // Instance variable

    public void setModel(String model) {
        this.model = model;
    }
}
```

3. Class Variables

Scope: Class variables are declared with the `static` keyword and are shared among all instances of a class. They belong to the class, rather than to any specific object.

Lifetime: They exist as long as the class is loaded in memory.

Example:

java

```
class Counter {
    static int count = 0;  // Class variable

    public void increment() {
        count++;
    }
}
```

Real-World Example: Building a Temperature Converter Using Different Data Types

Let's apply what we've learned about Java's data types and variables by creating a simple **temperature converter** program that converts temperatures between Celsius, Fahrenheit, and Kelvin.

Temperature Converter Program:
java

```
import java.util.Scanner;  // Import Scanner
class to read user input

public class TemperatureConverter {

    // Method to convert Celsius to Fahrenheit
```

44

```java
public            static          double
celsiusToFahrenheit(double celsius) {
      return (celsius * 9/5) + 32;
    }


    // Method to convert Celsius to Kelvin
    public static double celsiusToKelvin(double
celsius) {
      return celsius + 273.15;
    }


    // Method to convert Fahrenheit to Celsius
    public            static          double
fahrenheitToCelsius(double fahrenheit) {
      return (fahrenheit - 32) * 5/9;
    }


    // Method to convert Fahrenheit to Kelvin
    public            static          double
fahrenheitToKelvin(double fahrenheit) {
      return (fahrenheit - 32) * 5/9 + 273.15;
    }


    // Method to convert Kelvin to Celsius
    public static double kelvinToCelsius(double
kelvin) {
      return kelvin - 273.15;
    }
```

45

```java
// Method to convert Kelvin to Fahrenheit
public static double
kelvinToFahrenheit(double kelvin) {
    return (kelvin - 273.15) * 9/5 + 32;
}


public static void main(String[] args) {
    Scanner scanner = new
Scanner(System.in);  // Create scanner object for
user input

    System.out.print("Enter temperature: ");
    double temperature =
scanner.nextDouble();  // Get temperature value
from user

    System.out.print("Enter unit (C for
Celsius, F for Fahrenheit, K for Kelvin): ");
    char unit = scanner.next().charAt(0);  //
Get temperature unit from user

    double result;

    // Convert based on user input
    switch (unit) {
        case 'C':
            result =
celsiusToFahrenheit(temperature);
```

```
                System.out.println(temperature +
" Celsius is " + result + " Fahrenheit.");
                result                    =
celsiusToKelvin(temperature);
                System.out.println(temperature +
" Celsius is " + result + " Kelvin.");
                break;
            case 'F':
                result                    =
fahrenheitToCelsius(temperature);
                System.out.println(temperature +
" Fahrenheit is " + result + " Celsius.");
                result                    =
fahrenheitToKelvin(temperature);
                System.out.println(temperature +
" Fahrenheit is " + result + " Kelvin.");
                break;
            case 'K':
                result                    =
kelvinToCelsius(temperature);
                System.out.println(temperature +
" Kelvin is " + result + " Celsius.");
                result                    =
kelvinToFahrenheit(temperature);
                System.out.println(temperature +
" Kelvin is " + result + " Fahrenheit.");
                break;
            default:
```

```
            System.out.println("Invalid
unit.");

            break;
    }


    scanner.close();  // Close the scanner to
prevent memory leaks
  }
}
```

Explanation:

- **Primitive Data Types**: The program uses `double` for temperature values since temperatures can have decimal values.

- **Methods**: We define separate methods for converting between Celsius, Fahrenheit, and Kelvin, making the code modular and reusable.

- **Switch Statement**: Based on the user's input for the unit, we perform the appropriate conversion.

Sample Output:

```
mathematica

Enter temperature: 25
```

```
Enter unit (C for Celsius, F for Fahrenheit, K
for Kelvin): C
25.0 Celsius is 77.0 Fahrenheit.
25.0 Celsius is 298.15 Kelvin.
```

Conclusion

In this chapter, we've learned about:

Primitive data types such as int, double, char, and boolean.

Non-primitive data types like String, Arrays, and Classes.

Type casting and conversions, which allow us to convert between different data types in Java.

Variable scope and lifetime, which help us understand how and where variables are accessible in our program.

By creating the **temperature converter** program, you've seen how different data types can be used in real-world applications to manipulate and process data. In the next chapter, we'll explore **control flow** in Java, learning how to make decisions in our code using conditionals and loops. Let's keep building on this solid foundation!

CHAPTER 4

CONTROL FLOW STATEMENTS: CONDITIONALS AND LOOPS

In this chapter, we will explore how to control the flow of execution in a Java program. **Control flow statements** allow your program to make decisions, repeat actions, and break out of loops when necessary. Understanding these statements is key to writing programs that can handle various conditions and perform tasks repeatedly. We'll cover **conditionals** like if, else if, and else, as well as **loops** like for, while, and do-while. Additionally, we'll discuss the switch-case statement and control flow keywords such as **break** and **continue**.

---

if, else if, and else Conditions

The most basic control flow statement in Java is the **if statement**, which allows a program to execute a block of code only if a certain condition is **true**. If the condition is **false**, the program skips the code inside the if block.

Basic Syntax:

```java
```

```java
if (condition) {
    // Execute if the condition is true
} else {
    // Execute if the condition is false
}
```

Example:

```java

int age = 20;

if (age >= 18) {
    System.out.println("You are an adult.");
} else {
    System.out.println("You are a minor.");
}
```

else if and else

You can chain multiple conditions together using else if, allowing the program to check several conditions in sequence.

```java

int score = 85;

if (score >= 90) {
    System.out.println("Grade: A");
} else if (score >= 80) {
    System.out.println("Grade: B");
} else if (score >= 70) {
```

51

```
    System.out.println("Grade: C");
} else {
    System.out.println("Grade: F");
}
```

if: Tests the first condition.

else if: Tests a new condition if the previous if was false.

else: Executes a block of code if none of the conditions are true.

Switch-case Statements

The **switch-case** statement is an alternative to using multiple if-else if conditions when you need to compare one variable against several possible values. It's useful when you have many options to check against a single variable.

Basic Syntax:
java

```
switch (expression) {
    case value1:
        // Code to execute if expression == value1
        break;
    case value2:
```

```
        // Code to execute if expression ==
value2
        break;
    default:
        // Code to execute if no case matches
}
```

expression: The variable or value being evaluated.

case: The value that the expression is compared to.

break: Ends the switch block once a match is found. Without break, the program will "fall through" and execute subsequent cases.

default: Optional; this block executes if no case matches the expression.

Example:

```java

char grade = 'B';

switch (grade) {
    case 'A':
        System.out.println("Excellent");
        break;
    case 'B':
        System.out.println("Good");
```

```
        break;
    case 'C':
        System.out.println("Average");
        break;
    default:
        System.out.println("Invalid grade");
}
```

Loops: for, while, and do-while

Loops allow you to execute a block of code multiple times. The three main types of loops in Java are for, while, and do-while.

1. The for Loop

The for loop is used when you know in advance how many times you need to execute a statement or a block of statements.

Basic Syntax:

java

```java
for (initialization; condition; update) {
    // Code to execute on each iteration
}
```

initialization: Typically used to define and set a loop variable.

condition: Checked before each iteration; if true, the loop continues.

update: Usually increments or decrements the loop variable after each iteration.

Example:

java

```
for (int i = 0; i < 5; i++) {
    System.out.println("Iteration: " + i);
}
```

This loop runs 5 times, printing the numbers 0 through 4.

2. The while Loop

The while loop is used when you want to execute a block of code as long as a certain condition is **true**.

Basic Syntax:

java

```
while (condition) {
    // Code to execute while condition is true
}
```

Example:

java

```
int i = 0;
while (i < 5) {
    System.out.println("Iteration: " + i);
    i++;    // Increment the variable to avoid
infinite loop
}
```

This loop also runs 5 times, printing the numbers 0 through 4.

3. The do-while Loop

The do-while loop is similar to the while loop, but it guarantees that the code inside the loop will execute at least once, even if the condition is false initially.

Basic Syntax:
java

```
do {
    // Code to execute
} while (condition);
```

Example:
java

```
int i = 0;
do {
    System.out.println("Iteration: " + i);
    i++;
} while (i < 5);
```

This loop behaves similarly to the `while` loop but always runs at least once.

Break and Continue Keywords

The **break** and **continue** keywords allow you to control the flow of loops more precisely.

break: Exits the loop completely, even if the condition is not met.

continue: Skips the current iteration and moves to the next iteration of the loop.

Example of `break`:

```java
```

```java
for (int i = 0; i < 10; i++) {
    if (i == 5) {
        break;  // Exit the loop when i is 5
    }
    System.out.println(i);
}
```

Output:

```
0
```

1

2

3

4

Example of continue:

java

```
for (int i = 0; i < 5; i++) {
    if (i == 2) {
        continue;  // Skip iteration when i is 2
    }
    System.out.println(i);
}
```

Output:

0

1

3

4

Real-World Example: Implementing a Simple Number-Guessing Game

Now, let's bring together what we've learned about **control flow statements** by creating a simple **number-guessing game**. The game will randomly choose a number between 1 and 100, and the user will try to guess the number. The program will guide the user by providing feedback on whether the guess is too high, too low, or correct.

```java
import java.util.Scanner;   // Import Scanner class for user input
import java.util.Random;   // Import Random class for generating random numbers

public class NumberGuessingGame {

    public static void main(String[] args) {
        Scanner scanner = new Scanner(System.in);   // Create scanner object
        Random random = new Random();   // Create random object

        // Generate a random number between 1 and 100
        int targetNumber = random.nextInt(100) + 1;
        int guess = 0;
        int attempts = 0;

        System.out.println("Welcome to the Number Guessing Game!");
```

```java
        System.out.println("Guess    a    number
between 1 and 100.");

        // Loop until the user guesses the
correct number
        while (guess != targetNumber) {
            System.out.print("Enter your guess:
");
            guess = scanner.nextInt();   // Get
user input for the guess
            attempts++;   // Increment attempts

            if (guess < targetNumber) {
                System.out.println("Too low! Try
again.");
            } else if (guess > targetNumber) {
                System.out.println("Too    high!
Try again.");
            } else {

System.out.println("Congratulations!    You've
guessed  the  number  in  " + attempts + "
attempts.");
            }
        }

        scanner.close(); // Close the scanner to
prevent memory leaks
    }
```

}

Explanation:

Scanner: Used to get user input.

Random: Used to generate a random target number between 1 and 100.

while loop: The loop continues until the user guesses the correct number.

if-else conditions: Used to check if the guess is too low, too high, or correct.

Attempts tracking: We count how many attempts the user has made before guessing the number correctly.

Sample Output:

```vbnet
Welcome to the Number Guessing Game!
Guess a number between 1 and 100.
Enter your guess: 50
Too low! Try again.
Enter your guess: 75
Too high! Try again.
Enter your guess: 60
```

```
Congratulations! You've guessed the number in 3
attempts.
```

Conclusion

In this chapter, we've learned about **control flow statements** in Java:

Conditionals: `if`, `else if`, and `else` statements that allow you to make decisions in your programs.

Switch-case: A more efficient way of handling multiple conditions that involve one variable.

Loops: `for`, `while`, and `do-while` loops to repeat actions until certain conditions are met.

Break and continue: Keywords that help control the flow inside loops, allowing you to exit early or skip certain iterations.

We also built a simple **number-guessing game** to demonstrate how to apply these concepts in a real-world scenario. In the next chapter, we'll explore **arrays and collections**, which will allow us to store and manage data more efficiently.

CHAPTER 5

ARRAYS AND COLLECTIONS IN JAVA

In this chapter, we'll explore how to store and manage collections of data in Java. **Arrays** and **collections** provide ways to organize multiple pieces of data, making it easier to work with large sets of information. Understanding how to use arrays and collections effectively is essential for writing scalable and efficient Java programs. We will begin with an introduction to **arrays**, dive into **multi-dimensional arrays**, and then explore the **Java Collections Framework** (List, Set, and Map). Lastly, we will apply these concepts to a **real-world example** of managing a collection of books using an `ArrayList` or `HashMap`.

Introduction to Arrays in Java

An **array** is a collection of variables that are of the same type, and it allows you to store multiple values in a single variable. Each element in an array is identified by an **index**, and the index of the first element is always 0.

Array Declaration and Initialization

To declare an array, you need to specify the data type of the elements and the number of elements the array will hold.

java

```
int[] numbers = new int[5];  // Declare an array
of integers with 5 elements
numbers[0] = 1;  // Assign values to the array
elements
numbers[1] = 2;
numbers[2] = 3;
numbers[3] = 4;
numbers[4] = 5;
```

Alternatively, you can initialize the array at the time of declaration:

java

```
int[] numbers = {1, 2, 3, 4, 5};  // Initialize
the array with values
```

Accessing Array Elements

You can access elements in the array using the index:

java

```
int firstElement = numbers[0];   // Access the
first element (1)
int thirdElement = numbers[2];   // Access the
third element (3)
```

Multi-Dimensional Arrays

A **multi-dimensional array** is an array of arrays. The most common type is a **2D array**, which can be thought of as a table with rows and columns.

Declaration and Initialization of 2D Arrays

A 2D array can be declared and initialized as follows:

```java

int[][] matrix = new int[3][3];   // A 3x3 2D array
(3 rows and 3 columns)
matrix[0][0] = 1;   // Assigning values to the 2D
array
matrix[0][1] = 2;
matrix[0][2] = 3;
matrix[1][0] = 4;
matrix[1][1] = 5;
matrix[1][2] = 6;
matrix[2][0] = 7;
matrix[2][1] = 8;
matrix[2][2] = 9;
```

Alternatively, you can initialize a 2D array with predefined values:

java

```
int[][] matrix = {
    {1, 2, 3},
    {4, 5, 6},
    {7, 8, 9}
};
```
Accessing 2D Array Elements

To access an element in a 2D array, specify both the row and column index:

java

```
int element = matrix[1][2];  // Access element in row 1, column 2 (6)
```

Introduction to Java Collections

The **Java Collections Framework** provides a set of classes and interfaces to handle data more flexibly. It includes a variety of collections like **Lists**, **Sets**, and **Maps**, each designed for different use cases.

1. List

A **List** is an ordered collection that allows duplicates. It's an interface, and common implementations include `ArrayList`, `LinkedList`, and `Vector`.

> **ArrayList**: A dynamic array that grows automatically as elements are added. It's the most commonly used List implementation.
>
> ```java
> List<String> fruits = new ArrayList<>();
> fruits.add("Apple");
> fruits.add("Banana");
> fruits.add("Orange");
> ```

2. Set

A **Set** is a collection that does not allow duplicate elements. It's typically used when you need to store unique items.

> **HashSet**: The most common implementation of Set, it does not maintain any order of the elements.
>
> ```java
> Set<String>    uniqueFruits    =    new
> HashSet<>();
> uniqueFruits.add("Apple");
> ```

67

```
uniqueFruits.add("Banana");
uniqueFruits.add("Apple");    // Duplicate
element is ignored
```

3. Map

A **Map** is a collection that stores key-value pairs, where each key is associated with exactly one value. Unlike a List or Set, a Map allows for fast retrieval of data using a key.

> **HashMap**: The most commonly used Map implementation that does not guarantee the order of keys.
>
> java
>
> ```java
> Map<String, String> bookAuthors = new
> HashMap<>();
> bookAuthors.put("Harry    Potter",    "J.K.
> Rowling");
> bookAuthors.put("1984", "George Orwell");
> ```

Working with ArrayList and HashMap

Now that we've covered the basic types of collections in Java, let's look at how to use **ArrayList** and **HashMap** to store and manage collections of data.

ArrayList

An `ArrayList` is a resizable array that allows you to store elements, retrieve them by index, and modify the list dynamically.

Common Operations on ArrayList:

Adding elements:

```java
ArrayList<String> books = new ArrayList<>();
books.add("To Kill a Mockingbird");
books.add("Pride and Prejudice");
books.add("The Great Gatsby");
```

Accessing elements:

```java
String book = books.get(1);  // Access the second element (index 1)
System.out.println(book);    // Outputs: Pride and Prejudice
```

Iterating through an ArrayList:

```java
java
```

69

```java
for (String book : books) {
    System.out.println(book);
}
```

Removing elements:

```java
java
```

```java
books.remove("The    Great    Gatsby");    //
Remove by value
books.remove(0);  // Remove by index
```

HashMap

A `HashMap` is a collection of **key-value pairs**. It is commonly used to store unique keys associated with specific values, allowing for efficient retrieval of data based on keys.

Common Operations on HashMap:

Adding key-value pairs:

```java
java
```

```java
Map<String,    String>  bookAuthors  =    new
HashMap<>();
bookAuthors.put("To  Kill  a  Mockingbird",
"Harper Lee");
bookAuthors.put("1984", "George Orwell");
```

```
bookAuthors.put("The   Great   Gatsby",   "F.
Scott Fitzgerald");
```

Accessing values by key:

```
java
```

```java
String  author  =  bookAuthors.get("1984");
// Retrieve the value associated with the
key
System.out.println(author);   // Outputs:
George Orwell
```

Iterating through a HashMap:

```
java
```

```java
for  (Map.Entry<String,  String>  entry  :
bookAuthors.entrySet()) {
    System.out.println(entry.getKey()  +  "
by " + entry.getValue());
}
```

Real-World Example: Storing a Collection of Books Using an ArrayList or HashMap

Let's apply what we've learned by creating a program that stores a collection of books. We'll use an `ArrayList` to store the book titles, and a `HashMap` to associate each book with its author.

71

Book Collection Example:

java

```java
import java.util.ArrayList;
import java.util.HashMap;
import java.util.Map;

public class BookCollection {

    public static void main(String[] args) {
        // Using ArrayList to store book titles
        ArrayList<String>    books    =    new
ArrayList<>();
        books.add("To Kill a Mockingbird");
        books.add("1984");
        books.add("The Great Gatsby");

        // Using HashMap to store books with
their authors
        Map<String, String> bookAuthors = new
HashMap<>();
        bookAuthors.put("To Kill a Mockingbird",
"Harper Lee");
        bookAuthors.put("1984",         "George
Orwell");
        bookAuthors.put("The Great Gatsby", "F.
Scott Fitzgerald");

        // Printing book titles
```

```
        System.out.println("Books      in      the
collection:");
        for (String book : books) {
            System.out.println(book);
        }

        // Printing books and their authors
        System.out.println("\nBooks    and    their
authors:");
        for (Map.Entry<String, String> entry :
bookAuthors.entrySet()) {
            System.out.println(entry.getKey()    +
" by " + entry.getValue());
        }
    }
}
```

Explanation:

ArrayList: We use an `ArrayList` to store a list of book titles. This allows for easy addition and retrieval of book names.

HashMap: We use a `HashMap` to store the relationship between book titles and authors. This provides efficient retrieval of an author based on a book title.

Sample Output:

73

```
vbnet


Books in the collection:
To Kill a Mockingbird
1984
The Great Gatsby

Books and their authors:
To Kill a Mockingbird by Harper Lee
1984 by George Orwell
The Great Gatsby by F. Scott Fitzgerald
```

Conclusion

In this chapter, we explored how to store and manage collections of data in Java using **arrays** and **collections**. We covered:

Arrays: How to declare, initialize, and work with arrays, including multi-dimensional arrays.

Java Collections Framework: How to use `List`, `Set`, and `Map` interfaces, with practical examples of `ArrayList` and `HashMap`.

Real-World Example: We built a **book collection** application to demonstrate how to use `ArrayList` and `HashMap` to store and organize data.

In the next chapter, we will dive deeper into **methods**, how to define them, and how to use **method overloading** to make your programs more modular and efficient. Let's continue to build on this foundation!

CHAPTER 6

METHODS IN JAVA

In this chapter, we will explore **methods** in Java, which are a fundamental concept for structuring your programs. Methods allow you to define reusable blocks of code that can perform specific tasks. You'll learn how to define methods, understand method parameters, return types, and scope. We'll also dive into **method overloading**, **recursion**, and **iterative solutions**, two important approaches for solving problems. By the end of this chapter, you'll understand how to write and use methods effectively to make your code more modular, readable, and efficient.

Defining Methods in Java

A **method** in Java is a block of code that performs a specific task. It is defined inside a class and can be called to execute the code within it. Methods in Java consist of the following parts:

Access modifiers (optional): Specifies who can access the method (`public`, `private`, `protected`).

Return type: Specifies what type of value the method will return (e.g., int, String, void for methods that don't return anything).

Method name: The name used to call the method.

Parameters (optional): Variables passed into the method to provide input data.

Method body: The code that defines what the method does.

Basic Syntax:
java

```
returnType methodName(parameterList) {
    // Method body
}
```

Example: Defining a Simple Method
java

```
public class MyClass {

    // Method that adds two numbers and returns
the result
    public static int addNumbers(int a, int b) {
        return a + b;  // Return the sum of a and
b
    }
```

```
    public static void main(String[] args) {
        int sum = addNumbers(5, 3);   // Calling
the method
        System.out.println("Sum: " + sum);   //
Outputs: Sum: 8
    }
}
```

Access Modifier: public allows the method to be accessed from anywhere.

Return Type: int indicates the method returns an integer.

Method Name: addNumbers is the name of the method.

Parameters: int a, int b are the two parameters that the method uses for input.

Method Body: The logic that adds the two numbers and returns the result.

Method Overloading

Method overloading in Java occurs when multiple methods have the same name but different parameter lists. The methods must have a different number of parameters or different types of parameters to distinguish them.

Key Points About Method Overloading:

Overloaded methods can have the same name, but the **parameter types** or **number of parameters** must differ.

The return type is not considered when distinguishing overloaded methods. You cannot overload a method by changing only its return type.

Example of Method Overloading:

java

```
public class Calculator {

    // Method to add two integers
    public int add(int a, int b) {
        return a + b;
    }

    // Overloaded method to add three integers
    public int add(int a, int b, int c) {
        return a + b + c;
    }

    // Overloaded method to add two double values
    public double add(double a, double b) {
        return a + b;
    }
```

```
public static void main(String[] args) {
    Calculator calc = new Calculator();
    System.out.println("Sum of 2 integers: "
+ calc.add(5, 3));              // Calls add(int,
int)
    System.out.println("Sum of 3 integers: "
+ calc.add(5, 3, 2));          // Calls add(int,
int, int)
    System.out.println("Sum of 2 doubles: "
+ calc.add(5.5, 3.3));         // Calls add(double,
double)
    }
}
```

Here, the add method is overloaded three times, each with a different parameter list:

The first method adds two integers.

The second method adds three integers.

The third method adds two double values.

Method Parameters, Return Types, and Scope

1. Method Parameters

Parameters are variables that are passed into a method to provide input values.

You can have multiple parameters of different types in a method.

Parameters act as **local variables** within the method.

2. Return Types

A method in Java can return a value of any data type (such as `int`, `String`, or `boolean`).

If a method does not return any value, the return type is **void**.

3. Scope of Variables

Local variables (including parameters) are declared within a method and can only be used within that method.

Instance variables (declared outside methods but inside a class) can be accessed throughout the class.

Recursion and Iterative Solutions

Recursion and **iteration** are two common ways of solving problems that involve repetitive tasks.

1. Recursion

Recursion is a process where a method calls itself to solve smaller instances of a problem. Recursive methods must have a **base case** to terminate the recursion; otherwise, they will run indefinitely.

Example of Recursion: Calculating Factorial

The **factorial** of a number is the product of all positive integers less than or equal to that number. For example, `factorial(5) = 5 * 4 * 3 * 2 * 1`.

```java
public class Factorial {

    // Recursive method to calculate factorial
    public static int factorial(int n) {
        if (n == 0) {
            return 1;  // Base case: factorial of
0 is 1
        } else {
            return n * factorial(n - 1);  //
Recursive case
        }
    }

    public static void main(String[] args) {
```

```
    int result = factorial(5);   // Calling
the recursive method
        System.out.println("Factorial of 5: " +
result);   // Outputs: 120
    }
}
```

2. Iterative Solution

An **iterative** solution uses loops (like `for` or `while`) to solve repetitive problems. The factorial of a number can also be computed using iteration.

Example of Iteration: Calculating Factorial
java

```java
public class Factorial {

    // Iterative method to calculate factorial
    public static int factorialIterative(int n)
{
        int result = 1;
        for (int i = 1; i <= n; i++) {
            result *= i;   // Multiply result by
i on each iteration
        }
        return result;
    }

    public static void main(String[] args) {
```

```
        int result = factorialIterative(5);   //
Calling the iterative method
        System.out.println("Factorial    of    5
(iterative): " + result);   // Outputs: 120
    }
}
```

Recursion is useful for problems that can be broken down into smaller sub-problems, like calculating Fibonacci numbers, solving mazes, and tree traversal.

Iteration is typically preferred when the problem involves repetitive tasks with a known number of iterations or when performance is a concern (since recursion can be memory-intensive).

Real-World Example: Writing a Method to Calculate Factorial Numbers

In this real-world example, we will write a method to calculate the **factorial** of a number, both iteratively and recursively. The factorial is often used in combinatorics and probability calculations, making it a useful concept in many applications.

Complete Example: Factorial Program (Iterative and Recursive)
java

```java
public class Factorial {

    // Recursive method to calculate factorial
    public static int factorialRecursive(int n)
{
        if (n == 0) {
            return 1;  // Base case: factorial of
0 is 1
        } else {
            return n * factorialRecursive(n - 1);
// Recursive case
        }
    }

    // Iterative method to calculate factorial
    public static int factorialIterative(int n)
{
        int result = 1;
        for (int i = 1; i <= n; i++) {
            result *= i;
        }
        return result;
    }

    public static void main(String[] args) {
        int number = 5;

        // Recursive factorial
```

```
        int            resultRecursive       =
factorialRecursive(number);
        System.out.println("Factorial   of   "   +
number + " (Recursive): " + resultRecursive);

        // Iterative factorial
        int            resultIterative       =
factorialIterative(number);
        System.out.println("Factorial   of   "   +
number + " (Iterative): " + resultIterative);
    }
}
```

Sample Output:

```
mathematica

Factorial of 5 (Recursive): 120
Factorial of 5 (Iterative): 120
```

Conclusion

In this chapter, we've learned how to:

Define methods in Java to perform specific tasks, making your code more modular and reusable.

Overload methods to use the same method name with different parameters, improving code clarity and flexibility.

Understand **method parameters, return types**, and **scope** to better manage data within methods.

Explore **recursion** and **iteration** as two approaches to solving problems, such as calculating the factorial of a number.

We've implemented both **recursive** and **iterative** methods to calculate factorials and explored the advantages of both approaches.

In the next chapter, we'll delve into **arrays and collections** in Java, which will further enhance our ability to store and manage data efficiently in our applications. Let's keep building on our Java skills!

CHAPTER 7

OBJECT-ORIENTED PROGRAMMING (OOP) CONCEPTS

In this chapter, we will introduce the foundational principles of **Object-Oriented Programming (OOP)** in Java. OOP is a programming paradigm based on the concept of **objects**, which can contain both data (fields) and code (methods). OOP is designed to model real-world systems and is the foundation for building scalable, reusable, and maintainable software. We will explore the core concepts of OOP, including **classes**, **objects**, **methods**, and the four key pillars of OOP: **encapsulation**, **abstraction**, **inheritance**, and **polymorphism**. By the end of this chapter, we will build a **real-world example**: a simple banking system that demonstrates these OOP concepts.

Introduction to OOP: Classes, Objects, and Methods

At the heart of OOP is the idea of **objects** and **classes**.

1. Classes and Objects

A **class** is a blueprint or template for creating objects (instances). It defines the properties (fields) and behaviors (methods) that objects created from the class will have.

An **object** is an instance of a class. It is a real entity that exists in memory, created using the class definition.

2. Methods

Methods define the behaviors of objects. They perform operations on the object's data (fields) and can also return values.

Example:

java

```java
class Car {
    // Fields (attributes)
    String model;
    int year;

    // Method (behavior)
    void startEngine() {
        System.out.println(model  +  "  engine
started.");
    }
```

```
}


public class Main {
    public static void main(String[] args) {
        // Creating an object of the class 'Car'
        Car myCar = new Car();
        myCar.model = "Toyota";
        myCar.year = 2021;

        // Calling the method 'startEngine' on
the 'myCar' object
        myCar.startEngine();    // Output: Toyota
engine started.
    }
}
```

In the example above:

Car is the class.

myCar is an object of the class Car.

The startEngine method is the behavior of the object.

Understanding Fields, Methods, and Constructors

1. Fields (Attributes)

Fields are variables defined inside a class. They represent the state or properties of the object. Each object can have different values for these fields.

2. Methods (Behaviors)

Methods are functions defined within the class. They describe the behavior of the object and can manipulate the object's fields.

3. Constructors

Constructors are special methods used to initialize new objects. They have the same name as the class and do not have a return type.

If no constructor is defined, Java provides a default constructor that initializes the fields with default values (e.g., `null` for reference types, `0` for numeric types).

Example of Constructor:

```java
java

class Car {
```

```java
    String model;
    int year;

    // Constructor to initialize fields
    Car(String model, int year) {
        this.model = model;
        this.year = year;
    }

    // Method to start the engine
    void startEngine() {
        System.out.println(model  +  "  engine
started.");
    }
}

public class Main {
    public static void main(String[] args) {
        // Creating an object of the class 'Car'
using the constructor
        Car myCar = new Car("Toyota", 2021);
        myCar.startEngine();   // Output: Toyota
engine started.
    }
}
```

In this example:

The constructor `Car(String model, int year)` initializes the object's `model` and `year` fields when a new `Car` object is created.

The Four Pillars of OOP

The main principles of OOP are **encapsulation, abstraction, inheritance**, and **polymorphism**. Let's explore each of these concepts in detail:

1. Encapsulation

Encapsulation is the concept of **bundling** the data (fields) and the methods that operate on the data into a single unit (class). It also involves restricting access to some of the object's components, which is achieved by using **access modifiers**.

Public: Accessible from anywhere.

Private: Accessible only within the same class.

Protected: Accessible within the same package and subclasses.

Example of Encapsulation:

java

```java
class Account {
    private double balance;  // Private field

    // Public method to access the private field
    public double getBalance() {
        return balance;
    }

    // Public method to modify the private field
    public void deposit(double amount) {
        if (amount > 0) {
            balance += amount;
        }
    }
}

public class Main {
    public static void main(String[] args) {
        Account account = new Account();
        account.deposit(500);   // Deposit money into the account
        System.out.println("Balance:    " + account.getBalance());   // Access balance using a public method
    }
}
```

In this example:

The `balance` field is **private** and cannot be accessed directly outside the `Account` class.

Public methods (`deposit` and `getBalance`) are used to **access** and **modify** the balance.

2. Abstraction

Abstraction involves hiding the **complexity** of the system and showing only the essential details. This is done by creating abstract classes or interfaces that define **what** an object can do, but not **how** it does it.

Abstract class: A class that cannot be instantiated and may contain abstract methods (methods without implementation).

Interface: A contract that defines a set of methods that the implementing class must provide.

Example of Abstraction:

java

```
abstract class Account {
    abstract void deposit(double amount);   //
Abstract method
}
```

```
class SavingsAccount extends Account {
    void deposit(double amount) {
        System.out.println("Depositing      "    +
amount + " into savings account.");
    }
}


public class Main {
    public static void main(String[] args) {
        Account        myAccount      =        new
SavingsAccount();
        myAccount.deposit(1000);      //  Output:
Depositing 1000.0 into savings account.
    }
}
```

In this example:

> The Account class is **abstract**, and the deposit method is
> defined but not implemented in the base class.

> The SavingsAccount class implements the deposit
> method, providing the actual behavior.

3. Inheritance

Inheritance allows one class (child or subclass) to inherit properties and behaviors from another class (parent or superclass). This helps in code reuse and establishing a hierarchy of classes.

Example of Inheritance:

java

```java
class Animal {
    void eat() {
        System.out.println("This    animal    eats
food.");
    }
}

class Dog extends Animal {
    void bark() {
        System.out.println("The dog barks.");
    }
}

public class Main {
    public static void main(String[] args) {
        Dog myDog = new Dog();
        myDog.eat();   // Inherited method from
Animal class
        myDog.bark(); // Method from Dog class
    }
}
```

In this example:

The Dog class **inherits** the eat method from the Animal class
and also defines its own method bark.

4. Polymorphism

Polymorphism allows one object to take many forms. It enables you to call the same method on different objects, and each object responds in its own way. The two types of polymorphism are:

Method Overloading: Multiple methods with the same name but different parameter lists.

Method Overriding: A subclass provides a specific implementation of a method defined in the superclass.

Example of Polymorphism (Method Overriding):

```java
class Animal {
    void sound() {
        System.out.println("Animal makes a sound.");
    }
}

class Dog extends Animal {
    @Override
    void sound() {
        System.out.println("Dog barks.");
    }
}
```

```java
class Cat extends Animal {
    @Override
    void sound() {
        System.out.println("Cat meows.");
    }
}


public class Main {
    public static void main(String[] args) {
        Animal myDog = new Dog();
        Animal myCat = new Cat();

        myDog.sound();  // Outputs: Dog barks.
        myCat.sound();  // Outputs: Cat meows.
    }
}
```

In this example:

The sound method is **overridden** in both the Dog and Cat classes to provide specific behaviors.

Despite using the Animal reference type, Java calls the overridden method in the respective subclass, demonstrating **runtime polymorphism**.

Real-World Example: Building a Simple Banking System with Classes for Accounts and Transactions

Now that we understand the core concepts of OOP, let's build a **simple banking system** that models bank accounts and transactions. We'll use **encapsulation**, **inheritance**, and **polymorphism** to design the system.

java

```java
// Base class representing a general bank account
class Account {
    private double balance;

    public Account(double initialBalance) {
        this.balance = initialBalance;
    }

    public double getBalance() {
        return balance;
    }

    public void deposit(double amount) {
        if (amount > 0) {
            balance += amount;
        }
    }

    public void withdraw(double amount) {
```

```java
        if (amount > 0 && amount <= balance) {
            balance -= amount;
        }
    }
}


// Derived class representing a savings account
class SavingsAccount extends Account {
    private double interestRate;

    public SavingsAccount(double initialBalance,
double interestRate) {
        super(initialBalance);
        this.interestRate = interestRate;
    }

    public void applyInterest() {
        double   interest   =   getBalance()   *
interestRate / 100;
        deposit(interest);
    }
}

public class Main {
    public static void main(String[] args) {
        SavingsAccount     account     =     new
SavingsAccount(1000, 5);   // Create a savings
account with an initial balance and interest rate
        account.deposit(500);
```

```
        account.applyInterest();        //    Apply
interest to the account
        System.out.println("Balance:       "    +
account.getBalance());   // Output  the  current
balance
    }
}
```

Explanation:

> The `Account` class uses **encapsulation** to protect the
> `balance` field.

> The `SavingsAccount` class **inherits** from `Account` and
> adds an additional feature for applying interest.

> Methods like `deposit` and `withdraw` encapsulate logic for
> managing money in an account.

Sample Output:

yaml

Balance: 1575.0

Conclusion

In this chapter, we explored the key concepts of **Object-Oriented Programming (OOP)** in Java:

Classes and Objects: Fundamental building blocks of OOP.

Fields, Methods, and Constructors: The core components that define the properties and behaviors of objects.

The Four Pillars of OOP:

> **Encapsulation**: Bundling data and methods together while restricting access to some components.

> **Abstraction**: Hiding the complexity of the system and exposing only the necessary details.

> **Inheritance**: Reusing code by creating a new class based on an existing one.

> **Polymorphism**: Allowing objects to take many forms, enabling flexibility in method usage.

We also built a **simple banking system** that demonstrates how to use these OOP concepts in real-world applications. In the next chapter, we will explore **exception handling** in Java, which is essential for managing errors and improving program reliability.

CHAPTER 8

CLASSES AND OBJECTS IN JAVA

In this chapter, we will dive deeper into **classes** and **objects** in Java, which are fundamental concepts in object-oriented programming (OOP). You will learn how to create and use classes, work with **constructors**, access **instance variables**, and define **instance and static methods**. We will also explore the use of the `this` keyword, which helps in referencing the current object. To demonstrate these concepts, we will model a **Student class** with attributes like name and grade, simulating a simple student management system.

Creating and Using Classes

A **class** in Java is a blueprint for creating objects. It defines the properties (fields or instance variables) and behaviors (methods) that the objects created from the class will have.

Basic Syntax of a Class:

```java

public class Student {
    // Instance variables (attributes)
    String name;
```

```
    int grade;

    // Constructor
    public Student(String name, int grade) {
        this.name = name;
        this.grade = grade;
    }

    // Method to display student information
    public void displayInfo() {
        System.out.println("Name: " + name + ",
Grade: " + grade);
    }
}
```

In this example:

Student is the **class** name.

name and grade are **instance variables**.

displayInfo() is a **method** that displays information about the student.

The Student(String name, int grade) is a **constructor** used to initialize the object.

Using the Class (Creating Objects):

To use the class, we need to create objects (instances of the class).

```java

public class Main {
    public static void main(String[] args) {
        // Creating a new Student object
        Student student1 = new Student("Alice",
90);
        student1.displayInfo();      // Output:
Name: Alice, Grade: 90

        Student student2 = new Student("Bob",
85);
        student2.displayInfo();      // Output:
Name: Bob, Grade: 85
    }
}
```

student1 and student2 are objects created using the Student class.

The displayInfo() method is called on each object to display their information.

Constructors and the this Keyword

Constructors

A **constructor** in Java is a special method that is called when an object is instantiated. It initializes the object's state. The

106

constructor has the same name as the class and doesn't have a return type.

Default Constructor: Java provides a default constructor if no constructors are defined. It initializes all fields to default values (e.g., `null` for objects, `0` for numbers).

Parameterized Constructor: A constructor that takes arguments and initializes the fields of an object with those values.

In the `Student` class above, the constructor `Student(String name, int grade)` is **parameterized** and initializes the `name` and `grade` fields.

The `this` Keyword

The `this` keyword refers to the current instance of the class. It is commonly used to refer to the instance variables of the class when there is a name conflict between the parameter and the instance variable.

Example:

```java
java
```

```
class Student {
    String name;
    int grade;

    // Constructor
    public Student(String name, int grade) {
        this.name = name;   // 'this.name' refers
to the instance variable, 'name' is the parameter
        this.grade = grade;    // 'this.grade'
refers to the instance variable
    }

    public void displayInfo() {
        System.out.println("Name: " + this.name
+ ", Grade: " + this.grade);
    }
}
```

In the constructor, this.name refers to the instance variable name, while the name parameter is used to pass the value to the instance variable.

Instance Variables and Methods

Instance Variables: Variables declared inside a class but outside any method. They define the properties of an object. Each object of the class has its own of these variables.

Example of Instance Variables:

java

```
class Student {
    String name;   // Instance variable
    int grade;     // Instance variable
}
```

    Instance Methods: Methods that operate on instance variables. They require an instance of the class to be called.

Example of Instance Method:

java

```
class Student {
    String name;
    int grade;

    public void setName(String name) {
        this.name = name;  // Set the name of the
current object
    }

    public void setGrade(int grade) {
        this.grade = grade;  // Set the grade of
the current object
    }
```

```
public void displayInfo() {
    System.out.println("Name: " + name + ",
Grade: " + grade);
    }
}
```

The method `setName` and `setGrade` are **instance methods** because they modify the state of the object.

Instance vs Static Methods

Instance Methods

Instance methods are methods that belong to an object. To call an instance method, you must first create an object of the class.

These methods can access and modify instance variables.

java

```
class Student {
    String name;

    public void setName(String name) {
        this.name = name;  // Instance method
    }
}
```

Static Methods

Static methods belong to the class itself, not instances of the class. They are called using the class name and can be called without creating an object.

Static methods can only access **static** variables and cannot access instance variables.

Example of Static Method:

```java

class Student {
    static int studentCount = 0;    // Static
variable

    public static void incrementStudentCount() {
        studentCount++;        // Static   method
modifying static variable
    }

    public void displayCount() {
        System.out.println("Total students: " +
studentCount);
    }
}

public class Main {
```

```
public static void main(String[] args) {
    Student.incrementStudentCount();        //
Static method called without creating an object
    Student.incrementStudentCount();        //
Increment count twice

    Student student1 = new Student();
    student1.displayCount();    // Instance
method called on the object
    }
}
```

In this example:

incrementStudentCount is a **static method** that modifies the studentCount variable, which is also **static**.

The static method can be called directly via the class name Student.incrementStudentCount(), without creating an object.

Real-World Example: Modeling a "Student" Class with Attributes Like Name and Grade

Let's build a **Student** class to demonstrate all the concepts we have learned so far. We will create a class that has **name**, **grade**, and **student ID** as attributes, and methods to set and display these values. We'll also use constructors to initialize the values when creating objects.

java

```java
class Student {
    String name;
    int grade;
    int studentId;

    // Constructor to initialize the student's
attributes
    public Student(String name, int grade, int
studentId) {
        this.name = name;
        this.grade = grade;
        this.studentId = studentId;
    }

    // Method to display the student's
information
    public void displayInfo() {
        System.out.println("Student ID:  " +
studentId + ", Name: " + name + ", Grade: " +
grade);
    }

    // Static method to print the number of
students (this is just for demonstration)
```

```java
    public static void printStudentCount(int count) {
        System.out.println("Total number of students: " + count);
    }
}

public class Main {
    public static void main(String[] args) {
        // Create Student objects
        Student student1 = new Student("Alice", 90, 101);
        Student student2 = new Student("Bob", 85, 102);

        // Display student information
        student1.displayInfo();    // Output: Student ID: 101, Name: Alice, Grade: 90
        student2.displayInfo();    // Output: Student ID: 102, Name: Bob, Grade: 85

        // Calling static method to print student count
        Student.printStudentCount(2);
    }
}
```

Explanation:

The `Student` class has three attributes: `name`, `grade`, and `studentId`.

The **constructor** initializes the object's attributes when a new `Student` object is created.

The **displayInfo()** method prints the student's details.

The **static method** `printStudentCount` is used to demonstrate a method that operates on static data (the total number of students).

Sample Output:

```yaml
Student ID: 101, Name: Alice, Grade: 90
Student ID: 102, Name: Bob, Grade: 85
Total number of students: 2
```

Conclusion

In this chapter, we have explored the essential concepts related to **classes** and **objects** in Java:

Creating classes and objects: We saw how to define classes and instantiate objects using constructors.

Instance variables and methods: We learned how to define instance variables (attributes) and methods (behaviors) to represent the state and actions of objects.

Instance vs Static methods: We distinguished between instance methods, which operate on individual objects, and static methods, which belong to the class.

The this keyword: We used the `this` keyword to refer to the current object and differentiate between instance variables and method parameters.

The **Student class example** illustrated how to model a real-world entity with attributes and behaviors, using constructors and methods. In the next chapter, we will delve into **exception handling** in Java to ensure that our programs can handle errors gracefully and improve their robustness. Let's keep building on our knowledge of Java!

CHAPTER 9

INHERITANCE AND INTERFACES

In this chapter, we will dive into two of the most important concepts in **Object-Oriented Programming (OOP)**: **Inheritance** and **Interfaces**. We will also explore **Polymorphism** and **dynamic method dispatch**, which allow Java to execute methods at runtime in a flexible way. By understanding these concepts, you will be able to create more modular and reusable code. To help clarify these concepts, we will build a **real-world example**: a class hierarchy for animals (with classes such as `Dog` and `Cat`).

Inheritance: Extending Classes and Overriding Methods

Inheritance is one of the core principles of OOP. It allows you to define a new class based on an existing class. The new class (child or subclass) inherits the fields and methods of the existing class (parent or superclass), making it easier to reuse code.

Extending Classes

To create a subclass, we use the `extends` keyword to indicate that the new class is inheriting from a parent class. The subclass can inherit **all** the non-private fields and methods of the parent class.

Basic Syntax:
java

```java
class ParentClass {
    // Fields and methods of the parent class
}

class SubClass extends ParentClass {
    // Additional fields and methods for the
subclass
}
```

Example: Inheritance in Action
java

```java
class Animal {
    // Field common to all animals
    String name;

    // Method common to all animals
    public void speak() {
        System.out.println(name + " makes a
sound.");
    }
```

118

```java
}

class Dog extends Animal {
    // Method specific to dogs
    public void speak() {
        System.out.println(name + " barks.");
    }
}

class Cat extends Animal {
    // Method specific to cats
    public void speak() {
        System.out.println(name + " meows.");
    }
}

public class Main {
    public static void main(String[] args) {
        Dog dog = new Dog();
        dog.name = "Rex";
        dog.speak();   // Output: Rex barks.

        Cat cat = new Cat();
        cat.name = "Whiskers";
        cat.speak();   // Output: Whiskers meows.
    }
}
```

In this example:

Animal is the parent class with a `speak` method that is common to all animals.

Dog and **Cat** are subclasses that **override** the `speak` method to provide their own behavior.

The **speak** method is **overridden** in both `Dog` and `Cat` classes to print different sounds.

Overriding Methods

Overriding occurs when a subclass provides a specific implementation of a method that is already defined in the superclass. To override a method, the method in the subclass must have the same name, return type, and parameters as the method in the superclass.

Interfaces: Implementing Interfaces in Java

An **interface** in Java is a contract that defines a set of methods that a class must implement. Unlike classes, interfaces cannot contain implementation details for methods (prior to Java 8). Instead, they only define the method signatures, and the implementing class provides the method's functionality.

Basic Syntax of an Interface:
java

```
interface Animal {
    void speak();  // Method signature, no body
}
```

Implementing an Interface

A class implements an interface using the `implements` keyword. The class must provide concrete implementations for all methods defined in the interface.

Example of Implementing an Interface:

java

```
interface Animal {
    void speak();  // Interface method with no
body
}

class Dog implements Animal {
    public void speak() {
        System.out.println("Dog barks.");
    }
}

class Cat implements Animal {
    public void speak() {
        System.out.println("Cat meows.");
    }
}
```

121

```java
public class Main {
    public static void main(String[] args) {
        Dog dog = new Dog();
        dog.speak();  // Output: Dog barks.

        Cat cat = new Cat();
        cat.speak();  // Output: Cat meows.
    }
}
```

In this example:

The `Animal` interface defines a `speak` method.

Both `Dog` and `Cat` classes **implement** the `Animal` interface and provide their own version of the `speak` method.

Why Use Interfaces?

Loose coupling: Interfaces allow for decoupling between the classes that implement them. You can write flexible and reusable code that doesn't depend on the specific implementation of methods.

Multiple inheritance: A class can implement multiple interfaces, which helps avoid some of the limitations of single inheritance in Java.

Polymorphism and Dynamic Method Dispatch

Polymorphism allows an object to take many forms. Specifically, it allows a method to behave differently depending on the object that invokes it. In Java, polymorphism is often implemented via **method overriding** and **dynamic method dispatch**.

Dynamic Method Dispatch

When you call a method on an object, Java determines at runtime which version of the method to execute. This is known as **dynamic method dispatch**.

java

```java
class Animal {
    public void speak() {
        System.out.println("Animal    makes    a
sound.");
    }
}

class Dog extends Animal {
    public void speak() {
        System.out.println("Dog barks.");
    }
}
```

123

```
class Cat extends Animal {
    public void speak() {
        System.out.println("Cat meows.");
    }
}

public class Main {
    public static void main(String[] args) {
        Animal myDog = new Dog();    // Animal
reference, Dog object
        Animal myCat = new Cat();    // Animal
reference, Cat object

        myDog.speak();    // Dog barks. (runtime
polymorphism)
        myCat.speak();    // Cat meows. (runtime
polymorphism)
    }
}
```

In this example:

myDog is an Animal reference pointing to a Dog object, and myCat is an Animal reference pointing to a Cat object.

At runtime, Java uses **dynamic method dispatch** to call the overridden method in the Dog or Cat class, depending on the actual object.

This is an example of **runtime polymorphism**, where the method to be executed is determined at runtime based on the actual object type.

Real-World Example: Creating a Class Hierarchy for Animals

Let's build a simple example using the concepts of **inheritance**, **interfaces**, and **polymorphism**. We will model a class hierarchy for animals, with classes like Dog, Cat, and Bird. Each class will extend a base class Animal and implement an interface Sound.

Animal Class Hierarchy Example:

java

```java
// Interface that defines a sound method
interface Sound {
    void makeSound();
}

// Parent class 'Animal' with common attributes
class Animal {
    String name;

    // Constructor to initialize the name
    public Animal(String name) {
        this.name = name;
    }
```

```java
    // Method to display animal's name
    public void displayInfo() {
        System.out.println("Animal: " + name);
    }
}


// Dog class extends Animal and implements Sound
interface
class Dog extends Animal implements Sound {
    public Dog(String name) {
        super(name);
    }

    @Override
    public void makeSound() {
        System.out.println(name + " barks.");
    }
}

// Cat class extends Animal and implements Sound
interface
class Cat extends Animal implements Sound {
    public Cat(String name) {
        super(name);
    }

    @Override
    public void makeSound() {
        System.out.println(name + " meows.");
```

```java
        }
}


// Bird class extends Animal and implements Sound
interface
class Bird extends Animal implements Sound {
    public Bird(String name) {
        super(name);
    }

    @Override
    public void makeSound() {
        System.out.println(name + " chirps.");
    }
}


public class Main {
    public static void main(String[] args) {
        // Creating objects for different animals
        Dog dog = new Dog("Rex");
        Cat cat = new Cat("Whiskers");
        Bird bird = new Bird("Tweety");

        // Using polymorphism to call makeSound
        dog.makeSound();  // Output: Rex barks.
        cat.makeSound();   // Output: Whiskers
meows.
        bird.makeSound();   // Output: Tweety
chirps.
```

127

```
        // Using displayInfo from Animal class
        dog.displayInfo();  // Output:  Animal:
Rex
        cat.displayInfo();  // Output:  Animal:
Whiskers
        bird.displayInfo();  // Output:  Animal:
Tweety
    }
}
```

In this example:

- The Sound interface defines a contract for making a sound, which is implemented by each animal class (Dog, Cat, Bird).

- Each animal class extends the Animal class and overrides the makeSound method, demonstrating **method overriding** and **polymorphism**.

- **Dynamic method dispatch** ensures that the correct version of makeSound is called based on the actual object (e.g., dog, cat, or bird).

Conclusion

In this chapter, we explored:

Inheritance: How a subclass can inherit properties and methods from a superclass, promoting code reuse and a clear hierarchical structure.

Interfaces: How interfaces define a contract that classes must follow, allowing for flexibility and decoupling between components.

Polymorphism: The ability for different classes to provide their own implementation of a method defined in a common superclass or interface, enabling flexible code that adapts at runtime.

Dynamic Method Dispatch: How Java determines at runtime which method to invoke based on the actual object type, enabling polymorphism.

We also built a real-world example of an **animal class hierarchy**, demonstrating inheritance, interfaces, and polymorphism in action. In the next chapter, we will explore **exception handling** in Java, which will help you manage errors and create more robust applications. Let's continue building our Java skills!

CHAPTER 10

EXCEPTION HANDLING IN JAVA

In this chapter, we will explore **exception handling** in Java, a crucial concept that allows you to deal with unexpected situations or errors in your programs. Exception handling helps to ensure that your program can handle runtime errors gracefully without crashing. We will cover key concepts such as **errors** and **exceptions**, the usage of **try-catch blocks**, **throwing exceptions**, creating **custom exceptions**, and the **finally block**. By the end of this chapter, you will be able to write programs that can handle and recover from errors effectively. We will also walk through a **real-world example** of writing a program that handles file reading errors gracefully.

Understanding Errors and Exceptions

In Java, **errors** and **exceptions** are two types of issues that can occur during program execution:

> **Errors**: These are typically serious problems that the program cannot recover from, such as `OutOfMemoryError`. Errors are usually not handled by the programmer.

Exceptions: These are conditions that the program can potentially recover from. They represent abnormal situations that arise during program execution, such as an invalid input or a file not found. Exceptions can be handled using **exception handling mechanisms**.

Java provides a robust **exception handling mechanism** to handle exceptions in a structured and controlled way, preventing the program from terminating abruptly.

Try-Catch Blocks and Throwing Exceptions

The basic structure for exception handling in Java involves the use of **try-catch** blocks. The code that might throw an exception is placed inside the `try` block, and if an exception occurs, it is caught and handled by one or more `catch` blocks.

Basic Syntax:
java

```
try {
    // Code that may throw an exception
} catch (ExceptionType1 e1) {
    // Handle exception of type ExceptionType1
} catch (ExceptionType2 e2) {
    // Handle exception of type ExceptionType2
} finally {
```

```
    // Code that will always execute, regardless
of exception
}
```

Example: Handling Division by Zero

java

```java
public class Main {
    public static void main(String[] args) {
        try {
            int result = 10 / 0;   // This will
cause an ArithmeticException
        } catch (ArithmeticException e) {
            System.out.println("Error:    Cannot
divide by zero.");
        } finally {
            System.out.println("This will always
be executed.");
        }
    }
}
```

In this example:

The try block contains code that may throw an exception (10 / 0).

The catch block handles the ArithmeticException and provides an error message.

The `finally` block is executed regardless of whether an exception occurred or not, making it ideal for cleanup tasks.

Throwing Exceptions

Sometimes, you may want to explicitly throw an exception using the `throw` keyword. This can be useful if you want to signal that something went wrong in your method and need to pass the error to the calling method.

Example: Throwing a Custom Exception

java

```
public class Main {
    public static void checkAge(int age) {
        if (age < 18) {
            throw                            new
IllegalArgumentException("Age   must   be   18   or
older.");
        }
    }

    public static void main(String[] args) {
        try {
            checkAge(16);  // This will throw an
exception
        } catch (IllegalArgumentException e) {
```

```
        System.out.println("Exception:   " +
e.getMessage());
        }
    }
}
```

Here:

The `checkAge` method checks if the age is below 18 and throws an `IllegalArgumentException` if it is.

The exception is caught in the `catch` block and a message is printed.

Creating Custom Exceptions

In some cases, you may want to create your own exception types to represent specific errors that are relevant to your application. Custom exceptions can be created by extending the `Exception` class (or a subclass of `Exception`).

Example: Custom Exception for Invalid Temperature

java

```
class    InvalidTemperatureException    extends
Exception {
    public    InvalidTemperatureException(String
message) {
```

```
        super(message);
    }
}


public class TemperatureConverter {
    public    static    void    setTemperature(int
temperature)  throws  InvalidTemperatureException
{
        if (temperature < -273) {    // Below
absolute zero is not possible
            throw                            new
InvalidTemperatureException("Temperature  cannot
be below absolute zero.");
        }
    }


    public static void main(String[] args) {
        try {
            setTemperature(-300);   // This will
throw InvalidTemperatureException
        } catch (InvalidTemperatureException e)
{
            System.out.println("Exception:  "  +
e.getMessage());
        }
    }
}
```

In this example:

`InvalidTemperatureException` is a custom exception class that extends `Exception`.

The `setTemperature` method throws this exception if the input temperature is below absolute zero.

The exception is caught and handled in the `catch` block.

Finally Block and Exception Chaining

The **finally block** is optional and is used to ensure that certain code is executed whether or not an exception occurs. It is typically used for cleanup tasks such as closing file streams, releasing resources, or closing database connections.

Exception Chaining: You can throw a new exception while retaining the original exception details by chaining exceptions. This is done by passing the original exception as the second argument when throwing a new one.

Example: Using Finally and Exception Chaining

java

```java
public class FileReaderExample {

    public static void readFile(String fileName)
throws Exception {
```

136

```java
        try {
            if (fileName == null) {
                throw                          new
NullPointerException("File    name    cannot    be
null.");
            }
            // Simulate reading a file
            System.out.println("Reading  file:  "
+ fileName);
        } catch (NullPointerException e) {
            throw   new   Exception("An   error
occurred  while  reading  the  file.",  e);    //
Exception chaining
        } finally {
            System.out.println("Closing      file
resources.");
        }
    }


    public static void main(String[] args) {
        try {
            readFile(null);   // This will throw
an exception
        } catch (Exception e) {
            System.out.println("Caught
exception: " + e.getMessage());
            e.printStackTrace();   // Print stack
trace of the original exception
        }
```

```
      }
}
```

In this example:

> **Exception Chaining** is demonstrated by catching a `NullPointerException` and throwing a new `Exception` that includes the original exception.

> The **finally block** ensures that resources (e.g., file streams) are always closed, even if an exception is thrown.

Real-World Example: Handling File Reading Errors Gracefully

In this real-world example, we will write a program that handles file reading errors. We will simulate file reading by using the `FileReader` class and handle potential errors, such as file not found or input/output issues, using **exception handling**.

File Reading with Exception Handling

java

```java
import java.io.FileReader;
import java.io.IOException;

public class FileReaderExample {
```

```java
    public static void readFile(String fileName)
{

        FileReader fileReader = null;

        try {
            fileReader              =           new
FileReader(fileName);    // Attempt to open the
file
            int character;
            while              ((character         =
fileReader.read()) != -1) {
                System.out.print((char)
character);   // Print the contents of the file
            }
        } catch (IOException e) {
            System.out.println("Error      reading
the file: " + e.getMessage());   // Handle file
I/O errors
        } finally {
            try {
                if (fileReader != null) {
                    fileReader.close();          //
Ensure file is closed
                    System.out.println("\nFile
closed successfully.");
                }
            } catch (IOException e) {
                System.out.println("Error
closing the file: " + e.getMessage());
```

```
        }
      }
   }


   public static void main(String[] args) {
      readFile("example.txt");   // Attempt to
read a non-existing file
   }
}
```

Explanation:

We use `FileReader` to attempt to open and read a file.

catch (IOException e) handles any file-related errors (like the file not being found).

finally ensures that the file stream is closed after the operation, whether the file was successfully read or an error occurred.

Sample Output (for a non-existent file):

vbnet

```
Error reading the file: example.txt (No such file
or directory)
Error closing the file: The process cannot access
the file because it is being used by another
process.
```

Conclusion

In this chapter, we explored the crucial concept of **exception handling** in Java:

Errors and exceptions: The difference between critical errors and exceptions that can be handled.

Try-catch blocks: The basic mechanism for handling exceptions.

Throwing exceptions: Using the `throw` keyword to signal errors explicitly.

Creating custom exceptions: Designing exceptions specific to your application needs.

Finally block: Ensuring cleanup tasks are always executed.

Exception chaining: Linking exceptions to retain the original error information.

We also built a **real-world file-reading example**, demonstrating how to handle **file-related errors** gracefully using exceptions.

In the next chapter, we will dive into **Java's Collection Framework** to further explore how to work with different types

141

of collections like `List`, `Set`, and `Map`. Let's continue building your Java expertise!

CHAPTER 11

JAVA COLLECTIONS
FRAMEWORK

In this chapter, we will explore the **Java Collections Framework** (JCF), which is a set of interfaces, implementations, and algorithms for handling collections of objects. It provides a unified architecture for storing and manipulating groups of data. We'll cover the basic collection types such as **Lists**, **Sets**, and **Maps**, along with useful utilities like **Iterators**, **Generics**, and the **Comparable interface**. Additionally, we will look at **sorting** and **searching** in collections. By the end of this chapter, you'll understand how to effectively work with different collection types in Java. We will also implement a **real-world example**: a to-do list application that uses a collection to store tasks.

Lists, Sets, and Maps

The **Java Collections Framework** includes several types of collections, each designed for specific use cases. The three most commonly used types are **Lists**, **Sets**, and **Maps**. Let's examine each one:

1. Lists

A **List** is an ordered collection that allows duplicates. It provides methods to access elements by their index and is commonly used when the order of the elements matters.

ArrayList: A resizable array implementation of the `List` interface. It provides fast access to elements but slower performance for insertion and deletion in the middle of the list.

LinkedList: A doubly-linked list implementation of the `List` interface. It provides fast insertion and deletion of elements but slower access to elements by index.

Example: ArrayList and LinkedList:

```java
import java.util.*;

public class ListExample {
    public static void main(String[] args) {
        // Using ArrayList
        List<String> arrayList = new ArrayList<>();
        arrayList.add("Task 1");
        arrayList.add("Task 2");
        arrayList.add("Task 3");
```

144

```
    // Using LinkedList
    List<String>     linkedList     =     new
LinkedList<>();
        linkedList.add("Task 4");
        linkedList.add("Task 5");

        System.out.println("ArrayList:     "    +
arrayList);
        System.out.println("LinkedList:     "    +
linkedList);
    }
}
```

2. Sets

A **Set** is a collection that does not allow duplicate elements. It is useful when you want to store unique elements.

HashSet: The most commonly used Set implementation. It is backed by a hash table and does not maintain any specific order of elements.

TreeSet: A Set implementation that maintains elements in a sorted order, using a red-black tree internally.

Example: HashSet and TreeSet:

```
java
```

```java
import java.util.*;

public class SetExample {
    public static void main(String[] args) {
        // Using HashSet
        Set<String> hashSet = new HashSet<>();
        hashSet.add("Apple");
        hashSet.add("Banana");
        hashSet.add("Apple"); // Duplicate, will
not be added

        // Using TreeSet
        Set<String> treeSet = new TreeSet<>();
        treeSet.add("Orange");
        treeSet.add("Apple");
        treeSet.add("Banana");

        System.out.println("HashSet:       "     +
hashSet);
        System.out.println("TreeSet (sorted):  "
+ treeSet);
    }
}
```

3. Maps

A **Map** is a collection of key-value pairs, where each key is unique and is associated with exactly one value. It is useful when you need fast access to data based on a key.

HashMap: The most commonly used Map implementation. It stores keys and values using a hash table, and the order of keys is not maintained.

TreeMap: A Map implementation that maintains the keys in a sorted order, using a red-black tree.

Example: HashMap and TreeMap:

```java
import java.util.*;

public class MapExample {
    public static void main(String[] args) {
        // Using HashMap
        Map<String, String> hashMap = new HashMap<>();
        hashMap.put("1", "Task 1");
        hashMap.put("2", "Task 2");

        // Using TreeMap
        Map<String, String> treeMap = new TreeMap<>();
        treeMap.put("2", "Task 2");
        treeMap.put("1", "Task 1");

        System.out.println("HashMap: " + hashMap);
```

```
        System.out.println("TreeMap (sorted): "
+ treeMap);
    }
}
```

Iterators, Generics, and Comparable Interface

1. Iterators

An **Iterator** is an object that allows you to traverse through a collection, such as a `List` or `Set`, and access each element in turn. It provides methods such as `hasNext()` and `next()` for iteration.

Example of Using Iterator:

java

```
import java.util.*;

public class IteratorExample {
    public static void main(String[] args) {
        List<String> tasks = new ArrayList<>();
        tasks.add("Task 1");
        tasks.add("Task 2");
        tasks.add("Task 3");

        Iterator<String> iterator = tasks.iterator();
        while (iterator.hasNext()) {
```

```
System.out.println(iterator.next());
        }
    }
}
```

2. Generics

Generics allow you to specify the type of elements that a collection will hold. This improves type safety and helps avoid `ClassCastException` errors by allowing compile-time type checking.

Example of Generics:

```java

import java.util.*;

public class GenericsExample {
    public static void main(String[] args) {
        List<String>    stringList    =    new
ArrayList<>();   // Generics ensure only String
can be added
        stringList.add("Task 1");
        stringList.add("Task 2");

        // stringList.add(3);   // Compile-time
error (cannot add an integer)
```

```
        for (String task : stringList) {
            System.out.println(task);
        }
    }
}
```

3. Comparable Interface

The **Comparable interface** allows objects to be compared for sorting. Classes that implement `Comparable` must define the `compareTo()` method to specify how the objects should be ordered.

Example of Using Comparable:

java

```
import java.util.*;

class Task implements Comparable<Task> {
    String name;
    int priority;

    public Task(String name, int priority) {
        this.name = name;
        this.priority = priority;
    }

    // compareTo method to sort by priority
    public int compareTo(Task other) {
```

```
        return      Integer.compare(this.priority,
other.priority);
    }
}


public class ComparableExample {
    public static void main(String[] args) {
        List<Task> tasks = new ArrayList<>();
        tasks.add(new Task("Task 1", 3));
        tasks.add(new Task("Task 2", 1));
        tasks.add(new Task("Task 3", 2));

        Collections.sort(tasks);      // Sorting
tasks by priority using compareTo()

        for (Task task : tasks) {
            System.out.println(task.name   +    "
(Priority: " + task.priority + ")");
        }
    }
}
```

Sorting and Searching in Collections

Sorting

In Java, you can sort collections in two ways:

Using Comparable: As we saw above, you can implement the Comparable interface to define the sorting order.

Using Comparator: A Comparator is a separate object used to define a custom sorting order.

Example of Sorting with Comparator:

```java
import java.util.*;

class Task {
    String name;
    int priority;

    public Task(String name, int priority) {
        this.name = name;
        this.priority = priority;
    }
}


class TaskPriorityComparator implements Comparator<Task> {
    public int compare(Task t1, Task t2) {
        return Integer.compare(t1.priority, t2.priority); // Compare based on priority
    }
}
```

```java
public class ComparatorExample {
    public static void main(String[] args) {
        List<Task> tasks = new ArrayList<>();
        tasks.add(new Task("Task 1", 3));
        tasks.add(new Task("Task 2", 1));
        tasks.add(new Task("Task 3", 2));

        // Sorting using a custom comparator
        Collections.sort(tasks,                  new
TaskPriorityComparator());

        for (Task task : tasks) {
            System.out.println(task.name   +   "
(Priority: " + task.priority + ")");
        }
    }
}
```

Searching

You can use `Collections.binarySearch()` to search for an element in a sorted collection. This is much faster than linear search (`for` loop) when dealing with large collections.

Example of Searching in a Sorted List:

```java
java

import java.util.*;
```

```java
public class SearchExample {
    public static void main(String[] args) {
        List<Integer>     numbers     =     new
ArrayList<>();
        numbers.add(10);
        numbers.add(20);
        numbers.add(30);
        numbers.add(40);
        Collections.sort(numbers);

        int                  index               =
Collections.binarySearch(numbers,    30);         //
Searching for 30
        System.out.println("Element    found    at
index: " + index);
    }
}
```

Real-World Example: Implementing a To-Do List App Using a Collection to Store Tasks

Now let's build a **to-do list** app using Java's `ArrayList` to store tasks. We'll allow the user to add tasks, mark them as completed, and display the list of tasks.

To-Do List Example:

java

```java
import java.util.*;

class Task {
    String name;
    boolean isCompleted;

    public Task(String name) {
        this.name = name;
        this.isCompleted = false;
    }

    public void completeTask() {
        this.isCompleted = true;
    }

    @Override
    public String toString() {
        return   name   +   (isCompleted   ?   "
(Completed)" : " (Pending)");
    }
}

public class ToDoListApp {
    public static void main(String[] args) {
        List<Task> taskList = new ArrayList<>();

        // Adding tasks
```

155

```
        taskList.add(new      Task("Finish     Java
assignment"));
        taskList.add(new Task("Buy groceries"));
        taskList.add(new Task("Call mom"));

        // Marking a task as completed
        taskList.get(0).completeTask();          //
Completing the first task

        // Displaying tasks
        System.out.println("To-Do List:");
        for (Task task : taskList) {
            System.out.println(task);
        }
    }
}
```

Sample Output:

```
java

To-Do List:
Finish Java assignment (Completed)
Buy groceries (Pending)
Call mom (Pending)
```

Conclusion

In this chapter, we explored the **Java Collections Framework** and its key components:

Lists, **Sets**, and **Maps**: We learned how to use `ArrayList`, `LinkedList`, `HashSet`, and `TreeMap` to store and manage collections of objects.

Iterators, **Generics**, and the **Comparable interface**: We discussed how to use iterators to traverse collections, how generics improve type safety, and how to implement custom sorting with `Comparable`.

Sorting and Searching: We demonstrated how to sort collections using `Comparable` and `Comparator`, and how to search efficiently with `binarySearch()`.

We also built a **real-world to-do list application** to showcase how to manage tasks using a collection. In the next chapter, we will explore **file handling in Java**, including reading from and writing to files. Let's keep building on our Java knowledge!

CHAPTER 12

JAVA STREAMS AND LAMBDA EXPRESSIONS

In this chapter, we will explore the power of **Java Streams** and **Lambda expressions**, which are key components of functional programming in Java. These features allow you to write more concise, expressive, and functional code. We will cover the basics of **streams**, including how to use common operations like map(), filter(), and reduce(), and introduce **lambda expressions** and **functional interfaces**. By the end of this chapter, you will be comfortable using streams and lambdas to simplify data manipulation tasks. We will also work through a **real-world example** of **filtering and sorting a list of employees** by their salary using Java Streams.

Introduction to Streams and Functional Programming

In traditional Java, many operations on collections require explicit loops and conditions to manipulate the data. However, with **streams**, you can perform operations on data in a more declarative and functional way. Streams allow you to process collections of objects in a functional style, using methods that can be chained together to perform complex operations.

What is a Stream?

A **stream** in Java is an abstraction that allows you to process sequences of elements (such as collections or arrays) in a functional way. Streams allow you to:

Perform operations like filtering, mapping, and reducing.

Chain operations in a readable and concise manner.

Avoid mutable state by operating on the data declaratively.

Streams come in two types:

Sequential Streams: Operations are performed in sequence on the data.

Parallel Streams: Operations are performed in parallel, potentially improving performance on large data sets.

Functional Programming in Java

Java, traditionally an object-oriented language, introduced functional programming concepts in Java 8. With the introduction of **lambda expressions** and **streams**, Java developers can write more concise and functional code.

Using map(), filter(), and reduce() Methods

These are three of the most commonly used methods in the Stream interface.

1. map() Method

The map() method is used to transform the elements of a stream. It applies a function to each element and returns a new stream with the transformed elements.

Example: Using map() to square each number in a list:

```java

import java.util.*;
import java.util.stream.*;

public class MapExample {
    public static void main(String[] args) {
        List<Integer> numbers = Arrays.asList(1, 2, 3, 4, 5);

        // Using map to square each element
        List<Integer>        squaredNumbers        = numbers.stream()

.map(n -> n * n)
```

```
.collect(Collectors.toList());
```

```
        System.out.println(squaredNumbers);    //
Output: [1, 4, 9, 16, 25]
    }
}
```

In this example:

The map() method applies the lambda expression (n -> n
  *   n) to each element of the stream, squaring each
  number.

2. filter() Method

The filter() method is used to select elements from a stream
that satisfy a specific condition. It takes a **predicate** (a function
that returns true or false) and filters out elements that do not
meet the condition.

Example: Using filter() to get even numbers:

```java

import java.util.*;
import java.util.stream.*;

public class FilterExample {
```

```
public static void main(String[] args) {
        List<Integer> numbers = Arrays.asList(1,
2, 3, 4, 5, 6);

        // Using filter to get even numbers
        List<Integer>        evenNumbers        =
numbers.stream()

.filter(n -> n % 2 == 0)

.collect(Collectors.toList());

        System.out.println(evenNumbers);        //
Output: [2, 4, 6]
    }
}
```

In this example:

The `filter()` method uses a lambda expression (`n -> n
% 2 == 0`) to select even numbers from the list.

3. reduce() Method

The `reduce()` method is used to combine the elements of a stream into a single result, such as a sum or a product. It takes two parameters:

An identity value, which is the initial value for the reduction.

A binary operator, which specifies how two elements of the stream should be combined.

Example: Using `reduce()` to sum all numbers in a list:

```java
import java.util.*;
import java.util.stream.*;

public class ReduceExample {
    public static void main(String[] args) {
        List<Integer> numbers = Arrays.asList(1, 2, 3, 4, 5);

        // Using reduce to calculate the sum
        int sum = numbers.stream()
                    .reduce(0, (a, b) -> a + b);

        System.out.println(sum);  // Output: 15
    }
}
```

In this example:

The `reduce()` method starts with an identity value of 0 and adds each element in the stream to accumulate the total sum.

163

Lambda Expressions and Functional Interfaces

Lambda Expressions

A **lambda expression** is a concise way to represent an anonymous function (i.e., a function without a name). Lambda expressions are used primarily to define the behavior of functional interfaces, which have just one abstract method.

Syntax of Lambda Expression:

java

```
(parameters) -> expression
```

Example:

java

```
// Lambda expression that prints a message
Runnable r = () -> System.out.println("Hello,
World!");
r.run();
```

Functional Interfaces

A **functional interface** is an interface with exactly one abstract method. Functional interfaces are used to represent lambda expressions. Common examples include `Runnable`, `Comparator`, and `ActionListener`.

164

Java provides the @FunctionalInterface annotation to indicate that an interface is intended to be functional, but this is optional.

Example of a Functional Interface:

java

```java
@FunctionalInterface
interface Calculator {
    int calculate(int a, int b);
}

public class LambdaExample {
    public static void main(String[] args) {
        // Using lambda expression to implement
the Calculator interface
        Calculator add = (a, b) -> a + b;
        System.out.println(add.calculate(5, 3));
// Output: 8
    }
}
```

Real-World Example: Filtering and Sorting a List of Employees by Their Salary Using Java Streams

In this example, we will model a list of employees and use Java Streams to filter out employees with a salary below a certain threshold and then sort them by their salary.

Employee Class:

java

```
class Employee {
    String name;
    double salary;

    public Employee(String name, double salary)
{
        this.name = name;
        this.salary = salary;
    }

    public String getName() {
        return name;
    }

    public double getSalary() {
        return salary;
    }

    @Override
```

```java
    public String toString() {
        return name + " - " + salary;
    }
}
```

Main Program Using Streams:

java

```java
import java.util.*;
import java.util.stream.*;

public class EmployeeStreamExample {
    public static void main(String[] args) {
        // List of employees
        List<Employee>        employees       =
Arrays.asList(
                new Employee("Alice", 75000),
                new Employee("Bob", 60000),
                new Employee("Charlie", 80000),
                new Employee("David", 50000),
                new Employee("Eve", 90000)
        );

        // Filtering and sorting employees by
salary
        List<Employee>    filteredEmployees    =
employees.stream()
                .filter(e -> e.getSalary() > 60000)
// Filter employees with salary > 60000
```

```
.sorted(Comparator.comparingDouble(Employee::ge
tSalary))  // Sort by salary
            .collect(Collectors.toList());

        // Printing the filtered and sorted list

filteredEmployees.forEach(System.out::println);
    }
}
```

Explanation:

> **Filtering**: The `filter()` method is used to select employees with a salary greater than `60,000`.

> **Sorting**: The `sorted()` method sorts the filtered employees by salary in ascending order.

> **Displaying Results**: The `forEach()` method prints the list of filtered and sorted employees.

Sample Output:

```
nginx

Alice - 75000.0
Charlie - 80000.0
Eve - 90000.0
```

Conclusion

In this chapter, we learned about the following key concepts:

Java Streams: A powerful way to process collections of data with functional-style operations such as `map()`, `filter()`, and `reduce()`.

Lambda Expressions: A concise way to represent functional interfaces, making your code more expressive and compact.

Functional Interfaces: Interfaces with a single abstract method, often used in conjunction with lambda expressions.

Sorting and Filtering: We demonstrated how to use streams to filter and sort data in a declarative and efficient way.

We also worked through a **real-world example** of filtering and sorting a list of employees by their salary, showing how to use streams for powerful data manipulation tasks. In the next chapter, we will explore **file I/O operations** in Java, which are essential for reading from and writing to files in your applications. Let's continue advancing our Java skills!

CHAPTER 13

FILE HANDLING IN JAVA

In this chapter, we will explore **file handling** in Java, which is essential for reading from and writing to files. Understanding how to work with files is fundamental for developing applications that need to store data persistently. We will cover common classes like `FileReader`, `BufferedReader`, and `FileWriter`, which are used for file I/O operations. Additionally, we will discuss **serialization and deserialization**, which allow you to save and load objects to and from files. To demonstrate these concepts, we will build a **real-world example**: a text-based address book that saves and loads contact information.

Reading from and Writing to Files

In Java, **file I/O** (input/output) operations are done using streams. Streams allow you to read and write data to files efficiently. Java provides two main types of streams:

Byte streams: Handle raw binary data (e.g., `FileInputStream`, `FileOutputStream`).

Character streams: Handle textual data (e.g., `FileReader`, `FileWriter`).

170

For most text-based file operations, **character streams** are preferred because they provide a convenient way to read and write text.

1. Reading from Files (FileReader and BufferedReader)

FileReader: Reads data from a file one character at a time.

BufferedReader: Buffers input from a `FileReader`, allowing for efficient reading of large amounts of text.

Basic Syntax for Reading from a File:

java

```
import java.io.*;

public class FileReaderExample {
    public static void main(String[] args) {
        try (BufferedReader reader = new
BufferedReader(new FileReader("sample.txt"))) {
            String line;
            while ((line = reader.readLine()) !=
null) {
                System.out.println(line);
            }
        } catch (IOException e) {
            e.printStackTrace();
        }
```

```
    }
}
```

In this example:

FileReader reads the file sample.txt.

BufferedReader wraps the FileReader to provide an efficient way to read lines of text.

2. Writing to Files (FileWriter)

FileWriter: Writes characters to a file, creating the file if it doesn't exist.

Basic Syntax for Writing to a File:

```java
import java.io.*;

public class FileWriterExample {
    public static void main(String[] args) {
        try    (FileWriter    writer    =    new
FileWriter("output.txt")) {
            writer.write("Hello, World!\n");
            writer.write("Welcome  to  Java  file
handling.");
        } catch (IOException e) {
            e.printStackTrace();
```

172

```
        }
    }
}
```

In this example:

FileWriter is used to write text to output.txt. If the file
doesn't exist, it will be created.

Serialization and Deserialization

Serialization is the process of converting an object into a byte
stream so that it can be saved to a file or transmitted over a
network. **Deserialization** is the reverse process: converting the
byte stream back into an object.

Java provides the **Serializable** interface, which marks a class
as capable of being serialized.

1. Serializing an Object

To serialize an object, you need to:

Implement the Serializable interface in the class.

Use ObjectOutputStream to write the object to a file.

Example: Serialization:

173

```java

import java.io.*;

class Contact implements Serializable {
    String name;
    String phoneNumber;

    public    Contact(String    name,    String
phoneNumber) {
        this.name = name;
        this.phoneNumber = phoneNumber;
    }
}

public class SerializationExample {
    public static void main(String[] args) {
        Contact contact = new Contact("John Doe",
"123-456-7890");

        try    (ObjectOutputStream    out    =    new
ObjectOutputStream(new
FileOutputStream("contact.ser"))) {
            out.writeObject(contact);          //
Serializing the Contact object
        } catch (IOException e) {
            e.printStackTrace();
        }
    }
```

```
}
```

In this example:

The `Contact` class implements `Serializable`, which allows it to be serialized.

The `ObjectOutputStream` writes the `Contact` object to a file called `contact.ser`.

2. Deserializing an Object

To deserialize an object, you can use the `ObjectInputStream` class, which reads the byte stream and reconstructs the original object.

Example: Deserialization:

```java
import java.io.*;

public class DeserializationExample {
    public static void main(String[] args) {
        try (ObjectInputStream in = new
ObjectInputStream(new
FileInputStream("contact.ser"))) {
```

```
        Contact    contact    =    (Contact)
in.readObject();  // Deserializing the Contact
object
        System.out.println("Name:    "    +
contact.name);
        System.out.println("Phone:    "    +
contact.phoneNumber);
    }        catch        (IOException        |
ClassNotFoundException e) {
        e.printStackTrace();
    }
  }
}
```

In this example:

> The `ObjectInputStream` reads the object from the `contact.ser` file and reconstructs the original `Contact` object.

Real-World Example: Creating a Text-Based Address Book to Save and Load Contacts

Now that we've covered the basics of file handling and serialization, let's build a **simple text-based address book**. This application will allow users to add contacts, save them to a file, and load them back.

AddressBook Class:

java

```java
import java.io.*;
import java.util.*;

class Contact implements Serializable {
    String name;
    String phoneNumber;

    public    Contact(String    name,    String
phoneNumber) {
        this.name = name;
        this.phoneNumber = phoneNumber;
    }

    @Override
    public String toString() {
        return "Name: " + name + ", Phone: " +
phoneNumber;
    }
}

public class AddressBook {
    private  static  final  String  FILE_NAME  =
"addressBook.ser";
    private List<Contact> contacts;

    public AddressBook() {
```

```java
        contacts = new ArrayList<>();
        loadContacts();   // Load contacts from
file when the app starts
    }

    public void addContact(String name, String
phoneNumber) {
        contacts.add(new            Contact(name,
phoneNumber));
        saveContacts();
    }

    public void listContacts() {
        if (contacts.isEmpty()) {
            System.out.println("No       contacts
found.");
        } else {

contacts.forEach(System.out::println);
        }
    }

    private void saveContacts() {
        try (ObjectOutputStream    out    =    new
ObjectOutputStream(new
FileOutputStream(FILE_NAME))) {
            out.writeObject(contacts);        //
Serialize the contacts list
        } catch (IOException e) {
```

```
        e.printStackTrace();
    }
  }


  private void loadContacts() {
      try (ObjectInputStream in = new
ObjectInputStream(new
FileInputStream(FILE_NAME))) {
          contacts = (List<Contact>)
in.readObject();  // Deserialize the contacts
list
      } catch (IOException |
ClassNotFoundException e) {
          System.out.println("No      previous
contacts found. Starting fresh.");
      }
  }


  public static void main(String[] args) {
      AddressBook addressBook = new
AddressBook();

      // Adding contacts
      addressBook.addContact("Alice",    "123-
456-7890");
      addressBook.addContact("Bob",  "987-654-
3210");

      // Listing contacts
```

```
        System.out.println("Address          Book
Contacts:");
        addressBook.listContacts();
    }
}
```

Explanation:

The Contact class is marked as Serializable, allowing us to save and load contact objects.

The AddressBook class maintains a list of contacts and provides methods to **add** contacts (addContact) and **list** contacts (listContacts).

Saving: The saveContacts method serializes the contacts list to a file (addressBook.ser).

Loading: The loadContacts method deserializes the contacts list from the file if it exists.

Running the Address Book Application:

When you run the application:

It adds a couple of contacts to the address book.

It saves these contacts to a file (addressBook.ser).

On subsequent runs, the contacts will be loaded from the file.

Sample Output:

```yaml
Address Book Contacts:
Name: Alice, Phone: 123-456-7890
Name: Bob, Phone: 987-654-3210
```

Conclusion

In this chapter, we learned the essential concepts of **file handling** in Java:

Reading from and writing to files using `FileReader`, `BufferedReader`, and `FileWriter`.

Serialization and deserialization for saving and loading objects.

Creating a text-based address book that demonstrates file I/O and object serialization in action.

By understanding how to work with files and serialize objects, you can build applications that save data persistently. In the next chapter, we will explore **multithreading** in Java, which allows you to execute multiple tasks concurrently for better performance.

CHAPTER 14

JAVA GUI PROGRAMMING: SWING AND JAVAFX

In this chapter, we will explore how to create **Graphical User Interfaces (GUIs)** in Java using two powerful libraries: **Swing** and **JavaFX**. We will cover the essential concepts of **event-driven programming**, how to work with different **layouts** and **components** (like buttons, text fields, panels), and guide you through building a **real-world example**: a simple calculator application with a graphical interface. By the end of this chapter, you will understand how to create interactive GUI applications in Java.

Introduction to Java Swing and JavaFX for GUI Programming

Java provides two popular libraries for building graphical user interfaces: **Swing** and **JavaFX**. Both libraries allow developers to create rich and interactive applications with a wide range of components and event handling mechanisms.

Swing:

Swing is a part of Java's standard library and has been the traditional GUI framework in Java for many years.

Swing is **lightweight**, meaning it doesn't rely on the operating system's native GUI components.

It provides a wide variety of components like buttons, labels, text fields, panels, and more.

Swing is built on top of the **Abstract Window Toolkit (AWT)**, but it offers more advanced features.

JavaFX:

JavaFX is a more modern GUI framework introduced by Oracle as part of Java 8 and is aimed at creating rich, interactive user interfaces.

It supports **2D and 3D graphics**, animations, and video, making it ideal for building more complex applications with richer user interfaces.

JavaFX uses an XML-based language called **FXML** for designing user interfaces, similar to how HTML is used for web development.

It is intended to replace Swing for new GUI applications, though Swing is still widely used.

Which One Should You Use?

Swing: If you are maintaining or working with older Java applications or need a simple GUI.

JavaFX: For modern applications that require rich UIs, animations, and multimedia features.

In this chapter, we will focus on **Swing**, as it is widely used and easy to integrate into most Java applications. However, we will also touch on **JavaFX** at the end of the chapter for those interested in more advanced GUI features.

Event-Driven Programming in Java

In **event-driven programming**, the program's flow is determined by user actions (events) such as clicks, key presses, or mouse movements. In Java, **listeners** and **event handlers** are used to handle events.

Key Concepts:

Events: Actions that occur, such as button clicks, mouse clicks, key presses, etc.

Listeners: Special objects that "listen" for specific events and respond to them.

Event Handling: The process of defining methods to handle events and bind them to GUI components.

Example: Button Click Event Handling

In Java Swing, you typically use **ActionListener** to handle button clicks. An `ActionListener` listens for actions (such as a button press) and performs a specific task when the event occurs.

```java
import javax.swing.*;
import java.awt.event.*;

public class ButtonClickExample {
    public static void main(String[] args) {
        // Create a JFrame (main window)
        JFrame frame = new JFrame("Button Click
Example");

        // Create a JButton
        JButton button = new JButton("Click Me");

        // Define an ActionListener for the
button
```

```
        button.addActionListener(new
ActionListener() {
            public                    void
actionPerformed(ActionEvent e) {

JOptionPane.showMessageDialog(frame,    "Button
clicked!");
            }
        });

        // Set up the layout and add the button
        frame.setLayout(new FlowLayout());
        frame.add(button);

        // Set default JFrame behavior and size
        frame.setSize(300, 200);

frame.setDefaultCloseOperation(JFrame.EXIT_ON_C
LOSE);
        frame.setVisible(true);
    }
}
```

In this example:

A JButton is created, and an **ActionListener** is added to it. When the button is clicked, the actionPerformed method is invoked, showing a pop-up message.

Layouts and Components: Buttons, Text Fields, Panels, and More

Java Swing offers various components that can be arranged in different **layouts**. Components are basic building blocks of the UI, like buttons, text fields, labels, checkboxes, and panels.

1. Components

Here are a few key Swing components:

JButton: A button that can trigger an action.

JTextField: A text field that allows users to input text.

JLabel: A label that displays text or images.

JPanel: A container for grouping other components.

JCheckBox: A checkbox for a boolean choice.

JRadioButton: A radio button, used for multiple mutually exclusive choices.

2. Layouts

Layouts control how components are arranged in a container. Common layouts include:

FlowLayout: Components are arranged from left to right.

BorderLayout: Divides the container into five areas: North, South, East, West, and Center.

GridLayout: Arranges components in a grid.

BoxLayout: Arranges components vertically or horizontally.

Example: Simple Layout with Buttons and Text Fields
java

```java
import javax.swing.*;
import java.awt.*;

public class SimpleLayoutExample {
    public static void main(String[] args) {
        // Create the frame (window)
        JFrame frame = new JFrame("Simple Layout
Example");

        // Set the layout to FlowLayout
        frame.setLayout(new FlowLayout());

        // Create components
        JTextField     textField     =     new
JTextField(15);  // 15 columns wide
        JButton button1 = new JButton("Button
1");
```

```
        JButton button2 = new JButton("Button
2");

        // Add components to the frame
        frame.add(textField);
        frame.add(button1);
        frame.add(button2);

        // Set default window behavior
        frame.setSize(300, 200);

frame.setDefaultCloseOperation(JFrame.EXIT_ON_C
LOSE);
        frame.setVisible(true);
    }
}
```

In this example:

The `JFrame` uses a **FlowLayout**, and components are added sequentially: a text field followed by two buttons.

Real-World Example: Building a Simple Calculator Application

Let's now build a simple **calculator** application with a graphical interface using Swing. This application will allow users to input two numbers and perform basic arithmetic operations (addition, subtraction, multiplication, and division).

Calculator Class Using Swing:

java

```java
import javax.swing.*;
import java.awt.*;
import java.awt.event.*;

public class SimpleCalculator {
    // Declare components
    private JFrame frame;
    private JTextField textField;
    private JButton[] numberButtons;
    private JButton addButton, subtractButton,
multiplyButton, divideButton, equalsButton,
clearButton;

    // Calculator logic
    private double num1 = 0, num2 = 0, result =
0;
    private String operator = "";

    public SimpleCalculator() {
        // Initialize frame and text field
        frame = new JFrame("Simple Calculator");
        textField = new JTextField(16);

        // Create number buttons
        numberButtons = new JButton[10];
        for (int i = 0; i < 10; i++) {
```

```
            numberButtons[i]          =          new
JButton(String.valueOf(i));

numberButtons[i].addActionListener(new
ActionListener() {
            public                    void
actionPerformed(ActionEvent e) {
                String        command        =
e.getActionCommand();

textField.setText(textField.getText()          +
command);
            }
        });
    }

    // Create operator buttons
    addButton = new JButton("+");
    subtractButton = new JButton("-");
    multiplyButton = new JButton("*");
    divideButton = new JButton("/");
    equalsButton = new JButton("=");
    clearButton = new JButton("C");

    // Operator button actions
    addButton.addActionListener(e          ->
setOperator("+"));
        subtractButton.addActionListener(e    ->
setOperator("-"));
```

```java
        multiplyButton.addActionListener(e    ->
setOperator("*"));
        divideButton.addActionListener(e      ->
setOperator("/"));
        equalsButton.addActionListener(e      ->
calculateResult());
        clearButton.addActionListener(e       ->
clearDisplay());

        // Layout setup
        JPanel panel = new JPanel();
        panel.setLayout(new GridLayout(4, 4));

        // Add number buttons
        for (int i = 1; i < 10; i++) {
            panel.add(numberButtons[i]);
        }
        panel.add(addButton);
        panel.add(numberButtons[0]);
        panel.add(equalsButton);
        panel.add(subtractButton);
        panel.add(multiplyButton);
        panel.add(divideButton);
        panel.add(clearButton);

        // Frame setup
        frame.add(textField,
BorderLayout.NORTH);
        frame.add(panel, BorderLayout.CENTER);
```

```java
        frame.setSize(300, 400);

frame.setDefaultCloseOperation(JFrame.EXIT_ON_C
LOSE);
        frame.setVisible(true);
    }


    // Set operator for arithmetic
    private void setOperator(String operator) {
        this.operator = operator;
        num1                                    =
Double.parseDouble(textField.getText());
        textField.setText("");
    }


    // Perform calculation
    private void calculateResult() {
        num2                                    =
Double.parseDouble(textField.getText());
        switch (operator) {
            case "+":
                result = num1 + num2;
                break;
            case "-":
                result = num1 - num2;
                break;
            case "*":
                result = num1 * num2;
                break;
```

193

```
        case "/":
                result = num1 / num2;
                break;
        }

textField.setText(String.valueOf(result));
    }

    // Clear the display
    private void clearDisplay() {
        textField.setText("");
        num1 = num2 = result = 0;
        operator = "";
    }

    public static void main(String[] args) {
        new SimpleCalculator();
    }
}
```

Explanation:

We use **Swing components** such as JTextField (for input) and JButton (for each calculator button).

The GridLayout is used to arrange the buttons in a 4x4 grid.

Event listeners are added to buttons to capture user input and perform calculations based on the selected operator.

The calculator supports **addition**, **subtraction**, **multiplication**, **division**, and **clear** functionality.

Conclusion

In this chapter, we learned about:

Java GUI programming using **Swing**: Building basic graphical interfaces with buttons, text fields, and panels.

Event-driven programming: Using listeners to handle events like button clicks.

Layouts and components: How to organize and display GUI components in different layouts.

Building a simple calculator: Using Swing components and event listeners to create an interactive calculator application.

We also touched briefly on **JavaFX**, which offers more advanced features and can be a powerful choice for building modern applications with rich UIs. In the next chapter, we will explore **multithreading** in Java to improve the performance of your applications by executing multiple tasks concurrently. Let's keep advancing our Java skills!

CHAPTER 15

WORKING WITH DATABASES IN JAVA

In this chapter, we will explore **Java Database Connectivity (JDBC)**, a technology that allows Java applications to interact with databases. We will cover how to establish a connection to a database, perform basic **CRUD operations** (Create, Read, Update, Delete), and integrate a database into a real-world application. By the end of this chapter, you will know how to connect a Java application to a **MySQL** or **SQLite** database and manipulate data stored in the database. Our real-world example will demonstrate how to build a simple **inventory management system** with database integration.

Java Database Connectivity (JDBC)

JDBC is a standard Java API for connecting and interacting with relational databases like **MySQL**, **SQLite**, and others. JDBC provides a set of interfaces and classes for performing database operations, such as executing SQL queries, inserting records, updating data, and deleting records.

Steps to Work with JDBC:

Load the Database Driver: JDBC requires a driver to connect to the database. For MySQL, the driver is `com.mysql.cj.jdbc.Driver`.

Establish a Connection: Use the `DriverManager` to get a connection to the database.

Create a Statement: Create a `Statement` or `PreparedStatement` object to execute SQL queries.

Execute SQL Queries: Use the `executeQuery()` method for `SELECT` statements and `executeUpdate()` for `INSERT`, `UPDATE`, and `DELETE` operations.

Process the Result: For `SELECT` queries, you can use a `ResultSet` to retrieve the results.

Close the Connection: Always close the `Connection`, `Statement`, and `ResultSet` objects to release database resources.

Connecting Java to a MySQL or SQLite Database

1. Connecting to a MySQL Database

To connect to a MySQL database, you need to:

Add the MySQL JDBC driver to your project.

Set up a connection URL that includes the database's address and credentials.

Here's an example of how to connect to a MySQL database:

```java

import java.sql.*;

public class MySQLExample {
    public static void main(String[] args) {
        try {
            // Load MySQL JDBC driver

Class.forName("com.mysql.cj.jdbc.Driver");

            // Establish a connection to the
database
            Connection          connection        =
DriverManager.getConnection(

"jdbc:mysql://localhost:3306/mydatabase",
"username", "password");

            // Create a statement object
            Statement          statement          =
connection.createStatement();
```

```
        // Execute a simple query to retrieve
data
        ResultSet        resultSet       =
statement.executeQuery("SELECT      *      FROM
products");

        // Process the result set
        while (resultSet.next()) {
            System.out.println("Product   ID:
" + resultSet.getInt("id"));
            System.out.println("Product
Name: " + resultSet.getString("name"));
            System.out.println("Price:   "  +
resultSet.getDouble("price"));
        }

        // Close the connection and statement
        resultSet.close();
        statement.close();
        connection.close();
    } catch (Exception e) {
        e.printStackTrace();
    }
  }
}
```

Explanation:

We load the MySQL JDBC driver with Class.forName().

We   establish   a   connection   using `DriverManager.getConnection()`.

We execute a `SELECT` query using the `Statement` object.

We process the results using the `ResultSet` object.

2. Connecting to an SQLite Database

SQLite is a lightweight, serverless database that is commonly used for smaller applications or when you don't need a full-scale relational database.

To connect to an SQLite database, you will need the SQLite JDBC driver. You can download it or include it via a build tool like Maven.

```java
import java.sql.*;

public class SQLiteExample {
    public static void main(String[] args) {
        try {
            // Load SQLite JDBC driver
            Class.forName("org.sqlite.JDBC");

            // Establish a connection to the
database (use a file-based SQLite database)
```

```
        Connection          connection          =
DriverManager.getConnection("jdbc:sqlite:invent
ory.db");

        // Create a statement object
        Statement           statement           =
connection.createStatement();

        // Execute a simple query to retrieve
data
        ResultSet           resultSet           =
statement.executeQuery("SELECT      *      FROM
products");

        // Process the result set
        while (resultSet.next()) {
            System.out.println("Product   ID:
" + resultSet.getInt("id"));
            System.out.println("Product
Name: " + resultSet.getString("name"));
            System.out.println("Price:   "   +
resultSet.getDouble("price"));
        }

        // Close the connection and statement
        resultSet.close();
        statement.close();
        connection.close();
    } catch (Exception e) {
```

```
        e.printStackTrace();
    }
  }
}
```

Explanation:

The process for connecting to SQLite is similar to MySQL but uses the SQLite JDBC URL (`jdbc:sqlite:inventory.db`), which points to the SQLite database file.

SQLite does not require a separate server like MySQL, and you specify the path to the database file directly.

CRUD Operations: Create, Read, Update, Delete

1. Create (INSERT)

To insert data into a database, use the `executeUpdate()` method. It works for all operations that modify the database, such as INSERT, UPDATE, and DELETE.

Example: Inserting a New Product into a MySQL Database:

java

```
String query = "INSERT INTO products (name, price) VALUES ('ProductA', 29.99)";
```

```
int               rowsAffected           =
statement.executeUpdate(query);
```

2. Read (SELECT)

You can read data from a database using `executeQuery()`, which returns a `ResultSet` containing the retrieved records.

Example: Retrieving Products from a MySQL Database:

```
java
```

```
ResultSet              resultSet              =
statement.executeQuery("SELECT      *      FROM
products");
while (resultSet.next()) {

System.out.println(resultSet.getString("name"))
;
}
```

3. Update (UPDATE)

You can update existing data in a table using an UPDATE query.

Example: Updating the Price of a Product:

```
java
```

```
String query = "UPDATE products SET price = 39.99
WHERE id = 1";
```

```
int              rowsAffected              =
statement.executeUpdate(query);
```

4. Delete (DELETE)

To delete data from a table, use the DELETE query.

Example: Deleting a Product:

```java
String query = "DELETE FROM products WHERE id =
1";
int              rowsAffected              =
statement.executeUpdate(query);
```

Real-World Example: Building a Simple Inventory Management System

Let's now combine all the concepts and create a **simple inventory management system** that allows users to:

Add new products to the inventory.

View all products.

Update product details (such as price).

Delete products from the inventory.

204

Inventory Management System Code:

java

```java
import java.sql.*;
import java.util.Scanner;

public class InventoryManagementSystem {
    private static Connection connection;
    private static Scanner scanner;

    public static void main(String[] args) {
        try {
            // Establish a connection to the
SQLite database
            connection                     =
DriverManager.getConnection("jdbc:sqlite:invent
ory.db");
            scanner = new Scanner(System.in);

            // Create products table if it
doesn't exist
            Statement        statement      =
connection.createStatement();
            statement.execute("CREATE  TABLE  IF
NOT EXISTS products (id INTEGER PRIMARY KEY, name
TEXT, price REAL)");

            // Main menu
            while (true) {
```

205

```
            System.out.println("Inventory
Management System");
            System.out.println("1.        Add
Product");
            System.out.println("2.       View
Products");
            System.out.println("3.     Update
Product");
            System.out.println("4.     Delete
Product");
            System.out.println("5. Exit");
            System.out.print("Choose        an
option: ");
            int choice = scanner.nextInt();
            scanner.nextLine();   // Consume
newline

            switch (choice) {
                case 1:
                    addProduct();
                    break;
                case 2:
                    viewProducts();
                    break;
                case 3:
                    updateProduct();
                    break;
                case 4:
                    deleteProduct();
```

```
                        break;
                    case 5:

System.out.println("Exiting...");
                        return;
                    default:

System.out.println("Invalid choice.");
                    }
                }
            } catch (SQLException e) {
                e.printStackTrace();
            }
        }


    private static void addProduct() {
        System.out.print("Enter    product    name:
");
        String name = scanner.nextLine();
        System.out.print("Enter    product    price:
");
        double price = scanner.nextDouble();

        try {
            String query = "INSERT INTO products
(name, price) VALUES (?, ?)";
            PreparedStatement    statement    =
connection.prepareStatement(query);
            statement.setString(1, name);
```

```
            statement.setDouble(2, price);
            statement.executeUpdate();
            System.out.println("Product    added
successfully.");
        } catch (SQLException e) {
            e.printStackTrace();
        }
    }

    private static void viewProducts() {
        try {
            String  query  =  "SELECT  *  FROM
products";
            Statement        statement        =
connection.createStatement();
            ResultSet          resultSet        =
statement.executeQuery(query);

            while (resultSet.next()) {
                System.out.println("ID:    "    +
resultSet.getInt("id"));
                System.out.println("Name:   "   +
resultSet.getString("name"));
                System.out.println("Price:  "  +
resultSet.getDouble("price"));
                System.out.println();
            }
        } catch (SQLException e) {
            e.printStackTrace();
```

```java
        }
    }


    private static void updateProduct() {
        System.out.print("Enter product ID to
update: ");
        int id = scanner.nextInt();
        scanner.nextLine();  // Consume newline

        System.out.print("Enter new price: ");
        double price = scanner.nextDouble();

        try {
            String query = "UPDATE products SET
price = ? WHERE id = ?";
            PreparedStatement statement =
connection.prepareStatement(query);
            statement.setDouble(1, price);
            statement.setInt(2, id);
            statement.executeUpdate();
            System.out.println("Product updated
successfully.");
        } catch (SQLException e) {
            e.printStackTrace();
        }
    }


    private static void deleteProduct() {
```

```
        System.out.print("Enter   product   ID   to
delete: ");
        int id = scanner.nextInt();

        try {
            String query = "DELETE FROM products
WHERE id = ?";
            PreparedStatement    statement    =
connection.prepareStatement(query);
            statement.setInt(1, id);
            statement.executeUpdate();
            System.out.println("Product   deleted
successfully.");
        } catch (SQLException e) {
            e.printStackTrace();
        }
    }
}
```

Explanation:

We use SQLite as the database and store product information in a `products` table.

The program provides a simple menu for adding, viewing, updating, and deleting products from the inventory.

Each operation is implemented using JDBC to interact with the database.

Sample Output:

```
pgsql


Inventory Management System
1. Add Product
2. View Products
3. Update Product
4. Delete Product
5. Exit
Choose an option: 1
Enter product name: Laptop
Enter product price: 800.00
Product added successfully.


Inventory Management System
1. Add Product
2. View Products
3. Update Product
4. Delete Product
5. Exit
Choose an option: 2
ID: 1
Name: Laptop
Price: 800.0
```

Conclusion

In this chapter, we:

Explored **JDBC** and learned how to connect Java to MySQL or SQLite databases.

Covered **CRUD operations** (Create, Read, Update, Delete) to manipulate data in a database.

Built a **real-world inventory management system** that interacts with a database to manage products.

By mastering JDBC, you can integrate Java applications with databases, making them capable of storing and retrieving persistent data. In the next chapter, we will explore **multithreading** in Java, which can improve the performance of your applications by allowing concurrent execution of tasks. Let's continue enhancing our Java skills!

CHAPTER 16

MULTITHREADING AND CONCURRENCY

In this chapter, we will dive into **multithreading** and **concurrency** in Java, essential concepts for improving the performance of applications that need to execute multiple tasks simultaneously. We will cover the basics of **creating and managing threads**, the challenges associated with **thread synchronization**, the usage of **ExecutorService** and **thread pools**, and common **concurrency issues** such as **deadlocks** and **race conditions**. To solidify your understanding, we will build a **real-world example**: a **multi-threaded download manager** that handles multiple file downloads simultaneously.

Creating and Managing Threads

In Java, a **thread** is the smallest unit of execution. A program can have multiple threads running concurrently, allowing for multitasking. You can create threads in two ways:

By extending the `Thread` class.

By implementing the `Runnable` interface.

213

1. Extending the Thread Class

You can create a thread by creating a subclass of the Thread class and overriding its run() method. The run() method contains the code that will be executed by the thread.

Example: Creating a thread by extending the Thread class:

```java
class MyThread extends Thread {
    public void run() {
        System.out.println("Thread            is
running!");
    }
}

public class ThreadExample {
    public static void main(String[] args) {
        MyThread thread = new MyThread();
        thread.start();  // Start the thread
    }
}
```

2. Implementing the Runnable Interface

Alternatively, you can implement the Runnable interface, which allows your class to define a run() method. This is often preferred because it allows your class to extend another class while still being able to run as a thread.

214

Example: Creating a thread by implementing the `Runnable` interface:

```java
class MyRunnable implements Runnable {
    public void run() {
        System.out.println("Thread            is
running!");
    }
}

public class RunnableExample {
    public static void main(String[] args) {
        MyRunnable      myRunnable      =      new
MyRunnable();
        Thread thread = new Thread(myRunnable);
        thread.start();  // Start the thread
    }
}
```

In both examples, the thread is started using the `start()` method. This invokes the `run()` method in the background.

Thread Synchronization

When multiple threads access shared resources, there can be issues such as **race conditions**, where the program's behavior

215

depends on the sequence or timing of threads. **Thread synchronization** ensures that only one thread can access a shared resource at a time, preventing these issues.

Synchronized Methods

You can make a method **synchronized** by using the `synchronized` keyword. This ensures that only one thread can execute the synchronized method at a time for a particular object.

Example: Synchronizing a method:

```java

class Counter {
    private int count = 0;

    public synchronized void increment() {
        count++;
    }

    public synchronized int getCount() {
        return count;
    }
}

public class SyncExample {
    public static void main(String[] args) {
        Counter counter = new Counter();
```

```java
// Thread 1
Thread t1 = new Thread(() -> {
    for (int i = 0; i < 1000; i++) {
        counter.increment();
    }
});

// Thread 2
Thread t2 = new Thread(() -> {
    for (int i = 0; i < 1000; i++) {
        counter.increment();
    }
});

t1.start();
t2.start();

try {
    t1.join();
    t2.join();
} catch (InterruptedException e) {
    e.printStackTrace();
}

System.out.println("Count:      "    +
counter.getCount());  // Output: Count: 2000
    }
}
```

In this example:

- The `increment()` and `getCount()` methods are synchronized to ensure that only one thread can update the `count` value at a time.

- **join()** is used to make the main thread wait until both `t1` and `t2` have finished executing.

ExecutorService and Thread Pools

Managing individual threads manually can become difficult and error-prone when working with a large number of threads. **ExecutorService** simplifies thread management by providing a thread pool.

A **thread pool** is a collection of worker threads that are ready to execute tasks. When you submit a task, the thread pool assigns a thread to execute it, reducing the overhead of creating new threads for each task.

Using ExecutorService to Manage Threads

You can create a thread pool using the `Executors` factory methods, like `newFixedThreadPool()`.

Example: Using `ExecutorService` for a thread pool:

```java
java

import java.util.concurrent.*;

public class ExecutorServiceExample {
    public static void main(String[] args) {
        ExecutorService    executorService    =
Executors.newFixedThreadPool(3);

        // Submitting tasks
        for (int i = 0; i < 5; i++) {
            executorService.submit(() -> {

System.out.println(Thread.currentThread().getName() + " is executing the task.");
            });
        }

        executorService.shutdown();            //
Gracefully shut down the executor service
    }
}
```

In this example:

A fixed thread pool of size 3 is created, meaning it will execute up to 3 tasks concurrently.

The `submit()` method is used to submit tasks to the thread pool.

Concurrency Issues: Deadlocks, Race Conditions

Concurrency issues arise when multiple threads access shared resources, leading to unintended behavior. The most common concurrency issues include **deadlocks** and **race conditions**.

1. Deadlock

A **deadlock** occurs when two or more threads are blocked forever because they are waiting for each other to release resources. This results in a situation where the threads cannot proceed.

Example of Deadlock:

java

```java
class DeadlockExample {
    private static final Object lock1 = new Object();
    private static final Object lock2 = new Object();

    public static void main(String[] args) {
        Thread t1 = new Thread(() -> {
            synchronized (lock1) {
```

```
                System.out.println("Thread     1:
Holding lock 1...");
                try { Thread.sleep(100); } catch
(InterruptedException e) {}
                synchronized (lock2) {
                    System.out.println("Thread
1: Holding lock 2...");
                }
            }
        });

        Thread t2 = new Thread(() -> {
            synchronized (lock2) {
                System.out.println("Thread     2:
Holding lock 2...");
                try { Thread.sleep(100); } catch
(InterruptedException e) {}
                synchronized (lock1) {
                    System.out.println("Thread
2: Holding lock 1...");
                }
            }
        });

        t1.start();
        t2.start();
    }
}
```

In this example, t1 holds `lock1` and waits for `lock2`, while t2 holds `lock2` and waits for `lock1`. Both threads are stuck in a **deadlock** and will never proceed.

2. Race Conditions

A **race condition** occurs when two or more threads access shared data concurrently and the result depends on the timing or sequence of access.

Example of Race Condition:

java

```java
class RaceConditionExample {
    private static int counter = 0;

    public static void main(String[] args) {
        Runnable task = () -> {
            for (int i = 0; i < 1000; i++) {
                counter++;    // Increment the
counter
            }
        };

        Thread t1 = new Thread(task);
        Thread t2 = new Thread(task);

        t1.start();
```

```
    t2.start();

    try {
        t1.join();
        t2.join();
    } catch (InterruptedException e) {
        e.printStackTrace();
    }

    System.out.println("Counter:      "    +
counter);   // Expected: 2000, but might be less
due to race condition
    }
}
```

In this example:

Both threads increment the `counter` 1000 times each.

Since the increment operation is not atomic, a **race condition** can occur where both threads read the same value and then write it back, leading to incorrect results.

To avoid race conditions, you can synchronize the increment operation.

Real-World Example: Implementing a Multi-Threaded Download Manager

Let's implement a **multi-threaded download manager** that downloads multiple files simultaneously. We will use **ExecutorService** to manage threads and perform download tasks concurrently.

DownloadManager Class:

java

```java
import java.io.*;
import java.net.*;
import java.util.concurrent.*;

public class DownloadManager {
    private static final ExecutorService
executorService                          =
Executors.newFixedThreadPool(4);   // 4 threads
for downloading

    public static void downloadFile(String
fileURL, String destination) {
        executorService.submit(() -> {
            try (InputStream in = new
URL(fileURL).openStream();
                FileOutputStream out = new
FileOutputStream(destination)) {
                byte[] buffer = new byte[1024];
```

224

```
                int bytesRead;
                while        ((bytesRead       =
in.read(buffer)) != -1) {
                    out.write(buffer,        0,
bytesRead);
                }
                System.out.println("Download
complete: " + destination);
            } catch (IOException e) {
                e.printStackTrace();
            }
        });
    }

    public static void main(String[] args) {

downloadFile("https://example.com/file1.jpg",
"file1.jpg");

downloadFile("https://example.com/file2.jpg",
"file2.jpg");

downloadFile("https://example.com/file3.jpg",
"file3.jpg");

downloadFile("https://example.com/file4.jpg",
"file4.jpg");
```

```
        // Shut down the executor service after
the downloads are finished
        executorService.shutdown();
    }
}
```

Explanation:

We use an **ExecutorService** with a fixed thread pool of 4 threads.

Each file download is submitted as a task to the executor, and the download is performed concurrently.

The **downloadFile()** method reads from the provided URL and writes the content to a file.

Conclusion

In this chapter, we covered:

Multithreading in Java, including how to create and manage threads using the `Thread` class and `Runnable` interface.

Thread synchronization using the `synchronized` keyword to avoid concurrency issues.

ExecutorService and thread pools for managing multiple threads efficiently.

Common **concurrency issues**, including **deadlocks** and **race conditions**, and how to handle them.

A **real-world example** of a **multi-threaded download manager**, demonstrating how to download multiple files concurrently.

In the next chapter, we will explore **Java Networking**, which enables your applications to communicate over the network. Let's continue building on our Java skills!

CHAPTER 17

NETWORKING IN JAVA

In this chapter, we will explore **networking in Java**, which allows you to create applications that communicate over a network, whether it be local (LAN) or over the internet. We will cover key concepts such as **sockets**, **TCP/IP** communication, and how Java supports client-server communication using **Java Sockets API**. Finally, we will build a **real-world example**: a basic **chat application** that allows two users to communicate over a network.

Introduction to Sockets and TCP/IP

A **socket** is one endpoint in a two-way communication link between two programs running on the network. It serves as the interface for sending and receiving data over the network. **TCP/IP (Transmission Control Protocol/Internet Protocol)** is the fundamental protocol suite that underpins most of the internet and local network communication.

Java provides the `java.net` package, which allows developers to work with sockets and handle network communication.

1. TCP/IP Protocol:

TCP: A connection-based protocol that ensures reliable data transfer between two devices. TCP manages packet ordering and error checking.

IP: The protocol responsible for routing packets to their destination across different networks.

2. Sockets in Java:

ServerSocket: A class that listens for incoming client connections and handles client requests.

Socket: A class that represents a connection to a server, allowing the client to send and receive data.

Client-Server Communication in Java

In a **client-server** model, the client makes requests to the server, which processes these requests and sends back responses. Java uses **TCP sockets** to facilitate this communication. The **ServerSocket** is used on the server-side to listen for incoming client requests, while the **Socket** is used on the client-side to establish a connection to the server.

Server Side:

ServerSocket is created to listen for incoming connections on a specified port.

When a connection is made, **accept()** is called, which returns a Socket object for communication with the client.

Client Side:

The **Socket** object is used to connect to the server at a specified host and port.

Sending and Receiving Data Over the Network

Once a connection is established between the client and the server, both can send and receive data using **InputStream** and **OutputStream**.

Client: The client sends data using the OutputStream of the Socket.

Server: The server reads data from the InputStream of the Socket and sends a response back.

Example of Sending and Receiving Data:

Client:

The client sends a request message (e.g., "Hello Server") to the server via the `Socket`'s `OutputStream`.

It receives a response from the server via the `InputStream`.

Server:

The server listens for the incoming connection and processes the client's request using the `InputStream`.

The server sends a response back to the client using the `OutputStream`.

Real-World Example: Building a Basic Chat Application Using Java Sockets

Let's now create a **basic chat application** that allows communication between a client and a server. The server will listen for incoming client connections, and the client will send and receive messages.

Server Code (Server-side application to listen for connections):

java

```java
import java.io.*;
import java.net.*;

public class ChatServer {
    public static void main(String[] args) {
        try (ServerSocket serverSocket = new
ServerSocket(1234)) {
            System.out.println("Server           is
listening on port 1234...");

            // Accept client connection
            Socket              socket              =
serverSocket.accept();
            System.out.println("Client
connected");

            // Create input and output streams
for communication with the client
            BufferedReader    input    =    new
BufferedReader(new
InputStreamReader(socket.getInputStream()));
            PrintWriter    output    =    new
PrintWriter(socket.getOutputStream(), true);

            String message;
            while ((message = input.readLine())
!= null) {
                System.out.println("Client says:
" + message);
```

```
            output.println("Server:    "    +
message);  // Echo message back to client
        }
    } catch (IOException e) {
        e.printStackTrace();
    }
  }
}
```

Client Code (Client-side application to send messages):
java

```java
import java.io.*;
import java.net.*;

public class ChatClient {
    public static void main(String[] args) {
        try     (Socket    socket    =    new
Socket("localhost", 1234)) {
            // Create input and output streams
for communication with the server
            BufferedReader    input    =    new
BufferedReader(new
InputStreamReader(System.in));
            PrintWriter    output    =    new
PrintWriter(socket.getOutputStream(), true);
            BufferedReader    serverInput    =    new
BufferedReader(new
InputStreamReader(socket.getInputStream()));
```

```
        System.out.println("Connected to the
server. Type your messages:");

        String userMessage;
        while          ((userMessage         =
input.readLine()) != null) {
            output.println(userMessage);  //
Send message to server
            String      serverResponse       =
serverInput.readLine();      //   Read   server's
response

System.out.println(serverResponse);     //  Print
server response
            }
        } catch (IOException e) {
            e.printStackTrace();
        }
    }
}
```

How the Chat Application Works

Server Side:

The server listens for incoming connections on port
1234 using a `ServerSocket`.

234

When a client connects, the server creates a `Socket` object to communicate with the client.

The server continuously reads messages from the client using an `InputStream` and echoes the messages back to the client.

Client Side:

The client connects to the server at `localhost` on port `1234` using a `Socket`.

The client sends user input to the server via the `OutputStream` and prints the server's responses received via the `InputStream`.

Running the Chat Application:

First, run the **server** code.

Then, run the **client** code in a separate terminal or IDE.

The client can now send messages, and the server will echo them back.

Sample Interaction:

```
arduino
```

235

```
Server (Console):
Server is listening on port 1234...
Client connected
Client says: Hello, Server!
Server: Hello, Server!

Client (Console):
Connected to the server. Type your messages:
Hello, Server!
Server: Hello, Server!
```

Handling Multiple Clients with Threads

In a real-world application, the server would need to handle multiple clients at the same time. This can be achieved by creating a new thread for each client connection.

Multi-Client Server:
java

```java
import java.io.*;
import java.net.*;

public class MultiClientChatServer {
    public static void main(String[] args) {
        try (ServerSocket serverSocket = new
ServerSocket(1234)) {
```

```
            System.out.println("Server          is
listening on port 1234...");

            while (true) {
                // Accept client connection
                Socket          socket          =
serverSocket.accept();
                System.out.println("New    client
connected");

                // Create a new thread to handle
client communication
                new
ClientHandler(socket).start();
            }
        } catch (IOException e) {
            e.printStackTrace();
        }
    }
}


class ClientHandler extends Thread {
    private Socket socket;
    private BufferedReader input;
    private PrintWriter output;

    public ClientHandler(Socket socket) {
        this.socket = socket;
        try {
```

237

```
            input   =   new   BufferedReader(new
InputStreamReader(socket.getInputStream()));
            output                    =            new
PrintWriter(socket.getOutputStream(), true);
        } catch (IOException e) {
            e.printStackTrace();
        }
    }


    public void run() {
        try {
            String message;
            while ((message = input.readLine())
!= null) {
                System.out.println("Client says:
" + message);
                output.println("Server:    "    +
message);  // Echo message back to client
            }
        } catch (IOException e) {
            e.printStackTrace();
        }
    }
}
```

In this multi-client server:

The server continuously listens for incoming client connections.

Each client connection is handled in a new thread, allowing the server to manage multiple clients concurrently.

Conclusion

In this chapter, we covered the following key concepts in Java networking:

Sockets: The foundation for client-server communication in Java.

TCP/IP Communication: How Java handles communication using the TCP/IP protocol.

Sending and Receiving Data: Using `InputStream` and `OutputStream` to exchange data between the client and server.

Building a Chat Application: A basic chat application that demonstrates how to use sockets for real-time communication.

Multi-threading for Multiple Clients: A method for handling multiple client connections concurrently using threads.

Networking is a critical aspect of modern software development, and mastering it allows you to build distributed applications that can communicate over networks. In the next chapter, we will dive deeper into **Java Security**, focusing on how to protect your applications and data. Let's continue expanding our Java expertise!

CHAPTER 18

WORKING WITH JSON AND XML IN JAVA

In this chapter, we will explore how to handle **JSON** (JavaScript Object Notation) and **XML** (Extensible Markup Language) data in Java. These data formats are commonly used for storing and exchanging data, especially in web services and APIs. We will cover how to **parse**, **manipulate**, and **generate** JSON and XML data in Java using various libraries. The chapter will include real-world examples like **building an API client** that consumes **JSON responses**.

Parsing and Manipulating JSON and XML Data

Both **JSON** and **XML** are used for data interchange between systems. **JSON** is lightweight, human-readable, and easy to parse, while **XML** is more verbose but offers a rich set of features such as data validation with schemas. In Java, you can manipulate both formats using various APIs and libraries.

JSON Parsing and Manipulation

JSON is widely used in APIs and web services due to its simplicity. Java provides several libraries for working with JSON data, including **Jackson** and **Gson**.

> **Jackson**: A powerful JSON library that can serialize Java objects to JSON and deserialize JSON to Java objects. It is widely used for high-performance processing.

> **Gson**: A Google library for converting Java objects to JSON and vice versa. It is easy to use and highly flexible.

XML Parsing and Manipulation

XML is more verbose than JSON, but it is still commonly used for data exchange, particularly in older systems and certain protocols (e.g., SOAP). Java provides **JAXP (Java API for XML Processing)** for XML parsing and manipulation.

JAXP includes:

> **DOM (Document Object Model)**: A tree-based parser that reads the entire XML file into memory.

> **SAX (Simple API for XML)**: An event-based parser that processes XML data as it is read, without storing the entire document in memory.

Using Libraries like Jackson and Gson for JSON

1. Jackson Library

Jackson is a powerful library for JSON processing in Java. It supports both **streaming** (low-level parsing) and **binding** (converting Java objects to JSON and vice versa).

To get started with Jackson, you need to add the Jackson library to your project. If you're using Maven, add the following dependencies to your pom.xml file:

xml

```xml
<dependency>

<groupId>com.fasterxml.jackson.core</groupId>
    <artifactId>jackson-databind</artifactId>
    <version>2.12.3</version>
</dependency>
```

Example: Parsing JSON with Jackson

java

```java
import com.fasterxml.jackson.databind.ObjectMapper;

public class JacksonExample {
    public static void main(String[] args) {
```

243

```java
        String   json   =   "{\"name\":\"John\",
\"age\":30, \"city\":\"New York\"}";

        ObjectMapper   objectMapper   =   new
ObjectMapper();
        try {
            // Convert JSON string to Java object
            Person            person           =
objectMapper.readValue(json, Person.class);
            System.out.println(person);
        } catch (Exception e) {
            e.printStackTrace();
        }
    }
}


class Person {
    private String name;
    private int age;
    private String city;

    // Getters and setters
    public String getName() { return name; }
    public void setName(String name) { this.name
= name; }

    public int getAge() { return age; }
    public void setAge(int age) { this.age = age;
}
```

```java
    public String getCity() { return city; }
    public void setCity(String city) { this.city
= city; }

    @Override
    public String toString() {
        return "Person{name='" + name + "', age="
+ age + ", city='" + city + "'}";
    }
}
```

In this example:

> We use **ObjectMapper** from Jackson to parse the JSON string and convert it to a `Person` object.

> Jackson automatically maps the JSON properties (`name`, `age`, `city`) to the corresponding fields in the `Person` class.

2. Gson Library

Gson is another popular library for working with JSON in Java. It is easy to use and provides good performance. Add the Gson dependency to your `pom.xml` file:

xml

```xml
<dependency>
```

245

```
        <groupId>com.google.code.gson</groupId>
        <artifactId>gson</artifactId>
        <version>2.8.8</version>
</dependency>
```

Example: Parsing JSON with Gson

java

```java
import com.google.gson.Gson;

public class GsonExample {
    public static void main(String[] args) {
        String   json   =   "{\"name\":\"Jane\",
\"age\":25, \"city\":\"London\"}";

        Gson gson = new Gson();
        // Convert JSON string to Java object
        Person   person   =   gson.fromJson(json,
Person.class);
        System.out.println(person);
    }
}

class Person {
    private String name;
    private int age;
    private String city;

    // Getters and setters
    public String getName() { return name; }
```

```java
    public void setName(String name) { this.name
= name; }

    public int getAge() { return age; }
    public void setAge(int age) { this.age = age;
}

    public String getCity() { return city; }
    public void setCity(String city) { this.city
= city; }

    @Override
    public String toString() {
        return "Person{name='" + name + "', age="
+ age + ", city='" + city + "'}";
    }
}
```

In this example:

> We use **Gson** to parse the JSON string and convert it to a `Person` object.

Reading and Writing XML with JAXP

The **Java API for XML Processing (JAXP)** provides tools to parse and generate XML in Java. JAXP supports both **DOM** (tree-based) and **SAX** (event-based) parsing methods.

Example: Parsing XML with JAXP (DOM)

java

```java
import javax.xml.parsers.*;
import org.w3c.dom.*;
import java.io.*;

public class JAXPExample {
    public static void main(String[] args) {
        try {
            // Parse XML file
            File file = new File("sample.xml");
            DocumentBuilderFactory factory =
DocumentBuilderFactory.newInstance();
            DocumentBuilder builder =
factory.newDocumentBuilder();
            Document document =
builder.parse(file);

            // Normalize XML structure

document.getDocumentElement().normalize();

            // Get the root element
            NodeList nodeList =
document.getElementsByTagName("employee");

            // Loop through employee nodes
```

```
        for    (int   i   =   0;   i   <
nodeList.getLength(); i++) {
            Node node = nodeList.item(i);
            if    (node.getNodeType()    ==
Node.ELEMENT_NODE) {
                Element element = (Element)
node;

                String        name        =
element.getElementsByTagName("name").item(0).ge
tTextContent();

                String        age        =
element.getElementsByTagName("age").item(0).get
TextContent();

System.out.println("Employee: " + name + ", Age:
" + age);
            }
        }
    } catch (Exception e) {
        e.printStackTrace();
    }
  }
}
```

In this example:

We use **DOM** parsing to read the sample.xml file.

We access the elements of the XML file using `getElementsByTagName()` and extract their text content.

XML Structure (`sample.xml`):

xml

```
<employees>
    <employee>
        <name>John</name>
        <age>30</age>
    </employee>
    <employee>
        <name>Jane</name>
        <age>25</age>
    </employee>
</employees>
```

Example: Writing XML with JAXP

To write XML data using JAXP, we use **TransformerFactory** and **Transformer** to convert Java objects to XML.

java

```
import javax.xml.parsers.*;
import javax.xml.transform.*;
import javax.xml.transform.dom.*;
import javax.xml.transform.stream.*;
import org.w3c.dom.*;
```

250

```java
public class WriteXMLExample {
    public static void main(String[] args) {
        try {
            // Create a new XML document
            DocumentBuilderFactory factory =
DocumentBuilderFactory.newInstance();
            DocumentBuilder builder =
factory.newDocumentBuilder();
            Document document =
builder.newDocument();

            // Create root element
            Element root =
document.createElement("employees");
            document.appendChild(root);

            // Create employee element
            Element employee =
document.createElement("employee");
            root.appendChild(employee);

            // Create name and age elements
            Element name =
document.createElement("name");

name.appendChild(document.createTextNode("John"
));
            employee.appendChild(name);
```

```java
            Element              age              =
document.createElement("age");

age.appendChild(document.createTextNode("30"));
            employee.appendChild(age);

            // Write XML to file
            TransformerFactory
transformerFactory                              =
TransformerFactory.newInstance();
            Transformer       transformer      =
transformerFactory.newTransformer();
            DOMSource       source      =      new
DOMSource(document);
            StreamResult     result     =     new
StreamResult(new File("output.xml"));
            transformer.transform(source,
result);

            System.out.println("XML file created
successfully.");
        } catch (Exception e) {
            e.printStackTrace();
        }
    }
}
```

In this example:

We create a new XML document and append elements using `createElement()` and `appendChild()`.

We use **Transformer** to write the XML content to a file.

Real-World Example: Building an API Client that Consumes JSON Responses

Let's build an API client that interacts with a **REST API** that returns data in **JSON** format. We will use **Jackson** to parse the JSON response and display the data.

API Client Code:

```java
import
com.fasterxml.jackson.databind.ObjectMapper;
import java.io.*;
import java.net.*;

public class APIClient {
    public static void main(String[] args) {
        try {
            // Send GET request to a public API
            URL        url        =        new
URL("https://jsonplaceholder.typicode.com/users
");
```

```java
        HttpURLConnection    connection    =
(HttpURLConnection) url.openConnection();
        connection.setRequestMethod("GET");

        // Read the response
        BufferedReader    reader    =    new
BufferedReader(new
InputStreamReader(connection.getInputStream()))
;
        StringBuilder    response    =    new
StringBuilder();
        String line;
        while ((line = reader.readLine()) !=
null) {
            response.append(line);
        }

        // Parse JSON response using Jackson
        ObjectMapper    objectMapper    =    new
ObjectMapper();
        User[]              users              =
objectMapper.readValue(response.toString(),
User[].class);

        // Print the users
        for (User user : users) {
            System.out.println(user);
        }
    } catch (Exception e) {
```

```
            e.printStackTrace();
        }
    }
}


class User {
    private String name;
    private String email;

    // Getters and setters
    public String getName() { return name; }
    public void setName(String name) { this.name
= name; }

    public String getEmail() { return email; }
    public    void    setEmail(String    email)    {
this.email = email; }

    @Override
    public String toString() {
        return   "User{name='"   +   name   +   "',
email='" + email + "'}";
    }
}
```

In this example:

We send a GET request to a public API (`https://jsonplaceholder.typicode.com/users`).

We parse the JSON response using **Jackson** and print out the names and emails of the users.

Sample Output:

```bash
User{name='Leanne                    Graham',
email='Sincere@april.biz'}
User{name='Ervin                    Howell',
email='Shanna@melissa.tv'}
...
```

Conclusion

In this chapter, we covered:

Working with JSON using libraries like **Jackson** and **Gson** to parse and generate JSON data.

Reading and writing XML using **JAXP** (DOM parsing) to process XML data.

Building a real-world API client that consumes JSON data using a REST API and processes it with **Jackson**.

Mastering these technologies allows you to easily handle data interchange in modern Java applications, especially when working with web services and APIs. In the next chapter, we will dive into **Java Security** to ensure your applications are protected against security threats.

CHAPTER 19

JAVA REFLECTION AND ANNOTATIONS

In this chapter, we will delve into two powerful features of Java: **Reflection** and **Annotations**. These tools allow developers to write more flexible, dynamic, and self-documenting code. Reflection provides the ability to inspect and modify classes, methods, and fields at runtime, while annotations enable metadata to be added to Java classes, methods, fields, and other elements of the code. By the end of this chapter, you will understand how to use both Reflection and Annotations effectively, and we will build a **real-world example**: a **simple framework to automatically generate reports from annotated classes**.

Introduction to Reflection in Java

Reflection in Java is the ability of a Java program to examine or modify the runtime behavior of applications running in the Java Virtual Machine (JVM). Reflection allows you to inspect classes, methods, fields, and constructors at runtime and even modify their values. While Reflection provides powerful features, it should be used with caution as it can impact performance and introduce security risks if misused.

Key Concepts of Reflection:

Inspecting Classes: You can obtain metadata about a class at runtime, including its methods, fields, constructors, and annotations.

Instantiating Objects: Reflection allows you to create new instances of classes dynamically using the `newInstance()` method.

Accessing Methods and Fields: You can access methods and fields of a class even if they are private.

Modifying Objects: You can modify the value of fields and invoke methods dynamically at runtime.

Basic Reflection Example

java

```
import java.lang.reflect.*;

public class ReflectionExample {
    public static void main(String[] args) {
        try {
            // Obtain the Class object for a
given class
```

```
        Class<?>              clazz         =
Class.forName("java.lang.String");

        // Get the class name
        System.out.println("Class Name: " +
clazz.getName());

        // Get the declared methods of the
class
        Method[]          methods         =
clazz.getDeclaredMethods();
        for (Method method : methods) {
            System.out.println("Method: " +
method.getName());
        }

        // Get the declared constructors
        Constructor<?>[]   constructors   =
clazz.getDeclaredConstructors();
        for  (Constructor<?>  constructor  :
constructors) {

System.out.println("Constructor:        "       +
constructor.getName());
        }

    } catch (ClassNotFoundException e) {
        e.printStackTrace();
    }
```

```
    }
}
```

Explanation:

Class.forName("java.lang.String") retrieves the `Class` object associated with the `String` class.

The `getDeclaredMethods()` method provides a list of all methods declared in the class, which we print.

Similarly, `getDeclaredConstructors()` provides the constructors of the class.

Using Annotations in Java

Annotations are metadata that provide information about code elements (such as classes, methods, fields) to the compiler or runtime environment. Annotations have no direct effect on the program's execution, but they can be processed by tools, frameworks, or libraries. Java provides several built-in annotations such as `@Override`, `@Deprecated`, and `@SuppressWarnings`.

261

Key Concepts of Annotations:

Defining Custom Annotations: You can create your own annotations to annotate various elements in your Java program.

Built-in Annotations: Java provides built-in annotations such as `@Override`, `@FunctionalInterface`, and `@Deprecated`.

Processing Annotations: Annotations can be processed at runtime or compile-time using tools like Reflection or annotation processors.

Defining and Using Custom Annotations
java

```
import java.lang.annotation.*;

@Retention(RetentionPolicy.RUNTIME)
@Target(ElementType.METHOD)
public @interface Reportable {
    String value() default "No description provided";
}

class ReportGenerator {
    @Reportable(value = "Generate monthly sales report")
```

```
    public void generateReport() {
        System.out.println("Generating
report...");
    }
}


public class AnnotationExample {
    public static void main(String[] args) {
        try {
            // Get the method
            Method          method          =
ReportGenerator.class.getMethod("generateReport
");

            // Check if the method has the
Reportable annotation
            if
(method.isAnnotationPresent(Reportable.class)) {
                Reportable    annotation    =
method.getAnnotation(Reportable.class);
                System.out.println("Report
description: " + annotation.value());
            }

            // Invoke the method
            method.invoke(new
ReportGenerator());

        } catch (Exception e) {
```

```
                    e.printStackTrace();
        }
    }
}
```

Explanation:

We define a custom annotation @Reportable, which can be
applied to methods. It contains a value field to provide a
description of the report.

The ReportGenerator class uses this annotation on its
generateReport() method.

In the AnnotationExample class, we use Reflection to
check if the generateReport() method is annotated
with @Reportable and print the description.

Reflection API for Inspecting Classes and Methods at Runtime

The Reflection API allows you to inspect and manipulate Java
classes, methods, and fields at runtime. This is useful for tasks
such as dynamically invoking methods, creating objects, or
accessing private fields.

Common Reflection Classes and Methods:

Class: Provides methods to get information about the class, such as its name, methods, and constructors.

`getMethods()`: Returns an array of `Method` objects representing all public methods of the class.

`getFields()`: Returns an array of `Field` objects representing all public fields of the class.

`getConstructors()`: Returns an array of `Constructor` objects for the class.

Method: Provides methods to invoke methods at runtime.

`invoke()`: Used to invoke the method.

Field: Provides methods to manipulate fields of a class.

`get()`: Gets the value of a field.

`set()`: Sets the value of a field.

Example: Using Reflection to Invoke Methods Dynamically

java

```
import java.lang.reflect.*;
```

```java
class MyClass {
    public void displayMessage() {
        System.out.println("Hello                    from
MyClass!");
    }
}


public class ReflectiveMethodInvocation {
    public static void main(String[] args) {
        try {
            // Get the class object
            Class<?> clazz = MyClass.class;

            // Get the method to invoke
            Method             method             =
clazz.getMethod("displayMessage");

            // Create an instance of the class
            Object             instance             =
clazz.getDeclaredConstructor().newInstance();

            // Invoke the method on the instance
            method.invoke(instance);
        } catch (Exception e) {
            e.printStackTrace();
        }
    }
}
```

Explanation:

We use Reflection to invoke the `displayMessage()` method of the `MyClass` class.

The method `getMethod()` is used to get the `Method` object for `displayMessage()`.

The `invoke()` method is used to call the method dynamically on the created instance.

Real-World Example: Building a Simple Framework to Automatically Generate Reports from Annotated Classes

Now, let's create a simple framework that reads **custom annotations** and generates a report automatically. The framework will inspect annotated methods using Reflection, gather the necessary information, and generate a report.

Reportable Annotation:

java

```
@Retention(RetentionPolicy.RUNTIME)
@Target(ElementType.METHOD)
public @interface Reportable {
    String    description()    default    "No
description";
}
```

Report Generator Class:

```java
import java.lang.reflect.*;

public class ReportGenerator {

    @Reportable(description = "Generate daily
report")
    public void generateDailyReport() {
        System.out.println("Generating    daily
report...");
    }

    @Reportable(description = "Generate weekly
report")
    public void generateWeeklyReport() {
        System.out.println("Generating    weekly
report...");
    }

    public void generateReports() {
        Method[]           methods           =
this.getClass().getDeclaredMethods();

        for (Method method : methods) {
            if
(method.isAnnotationPresent(Reportable.class)) {
```

```
                Reportable      reportable      =
method.getAnnotation(Reportable.class);
                System.out.println("Report
Description: " + reportable.description());
                try {
                    method.invoke(this);        //
Call the method
                } catch (Exception e) {
                    e.printStackTrace();
                }
            }
        }
    }
}


public class ReportFramework {
    public static void main(String[] args) {
        ReportGenerator  reportGenerator  =  new
ReportGenerator();
        reportGenerator.generateReports();
    }
}
```

Explanation:

The Reportable annotation is applied to the generateDailyReport() and generateWeeklyReport() methods.

The `generateReports()` method uses Reflection to inspect all methods of the `ReportGenerator` class. It checks if a method is annotated with `@Reportable` and prints the description from the annotation before invoking the method.

Output:

yaml

```
Report Description: Generate daily report
Generating daily report...
Report Description: Generate weekly report
Generating weekly report...
```

Conclusion

In this chapter, we covered the following key concepts:

Reflection in Java, allowing us to inspect and manipulate classes, methods, fields, and constructors at runtime.

Annotations, which provide metadata for classes, methods, and other code elements. We also explored how to define and use custom annotations.

A **real-world example** where we built a framework that automatically generates reports from annotated classes using Reflection.

Reflection and annotations are powerful tools for making Java applications more flexible and dynamic. In the next chapter, we will explore **Java Streams** and their advanced capabilities, helping you write more efficient and declarative code. Let's continue improving our Java skills!

CHAPTER 20

UNIT TESTING WITH JUNIT

In this chapter, we will explore **unit testing** in Java using **JUnit**, one of the most widely used frameworks for testing Java applications. Unit testing helps ensure that individual parts (or "units") of an application work correctly. Writing unit tests can catch errors early in the development process and improve the reliability of your code. We will cover how to write unit tests, test methods and classes, and the importance of **test-driven development (TDD)**. Finally, we will write test cases for a **user authentication system** to demonstrate practical testing concepts.

Writing Unit Tests in Java Using JUnit

JUnit is a **unit testing framework** for Java, allowing developers to write and run tests to verify that their code behaves as expected. JUnit supports **annotations**, **assertions**, and test runners, making it easy to create and manage tests.

Setting Up JUnit

To use JUnit in your Java project, you will need to add it as a dependency. If you're using Maven, you can add the following dependency to your pom.xml file:

xml

```
<dependency>
    <groupId>org.junit.jupiter</groupId>
    <artifactId>junit-jupiter-api</artifactId>
    <version>5.7.1</version>
    <scope>test</scope>
</dependency>
<dependency>
    <groupId>org.junit.jupiter</groupId>
    <artifactId>junit-jupiter-
engine</artifactId>
    <version>5.7.1</version>
    <scope>test</scope>
</dependency>
```

JUnit has evolved over time, and **JUnit 5** (also called **Jupiter**) is the latest version, which includes a more flexible and powerful API for writing and running tests.

JUnit Annotations

JUnit 5 uses several important annotations to identify test methods, setup methods, and teardown methods:

@Test: Marks a method as a test method.

@BeforeEach: Runs before each test method is executed (used for setup).

@AfterEach: Runs after each test method is executed (used for cleanup).

@BeforeAll: Runs once before any test methods are executed (used for global setup).

@AfterAll: Runs once after all test methods are executed (used for global cleanup).

Testing Methods, Classes, and Integration Testing

JUnit allows us to test **individual methods** (unit tests), **classes** (grouping tests for related methods), and even **integrated systems** (testing interactions between components).

1. Testing Methods

Unit tests typically involve testing individual methods to ensure they produce the correct output for given inputs.

Example: Testing a Method Let's say we have a simple Calculator class with an add() method:

java

```java
public class Calculator {
    public int add(int a, int b) {
        return a + b;
```

274

```
    }
}
```

Now, let's write a unit test for the add() method using JUnit:

```java

import org.junit.jupiter.api.Test;
import                              static
org.junit.jupiter.api.Assertions.*;

public class CalculatorTest {

    @Test
    public void testAdd() {
        Calculator    calculator    =    new
Calculator();
        int result = calculator.add(2, 3);
        assertEquals(5,  result,  "2 + 3 should
equal 5");
    }
}
```

In this example:

We use the @Test annotation to mark the testAdd() method
as a test case.

The assertEquals() method checks if the result from
add() is correct.

275

2. Testing Classes

You can write multiple tests for the methods of a class to verify that the entire class behaves as expected.

java

```java
public class MathOperations {
    public int multiply(int a, int b) {
        return a * b;
    }

    public int divide(int a, int b) {
        if (b == 0) {
            throw                               new
ArithmeticException("Cannot divide by zero");
        }
        return a / b;
    }
}
```

Example: Testing the MathOperations Class

java

```java
import org.junit.jupiter.api.Test;
import                                      static
org.junit.jupiter.api.Assertions.*;

public class MathOperationsTest {
```

```
    @Test
    public void testMultiply() {
        MathOperations    operations    =    new
MathOperations();
        int result = operations.multiply(3, 4);
        assertEquals(12, result);
    }

    @Test
    public void testDivide() {
        MathOperations    operations    =    new
MathOperations();
        int result = operations.divide(10, 2);
        assertEquals(5, result);
    }

    @Test
    public void testDivideByZero() {
        MathOperations    operations    =    new
MathOperations();
        assertThrows(ArithmeticException.class,
() -> operations.divide(10, 0));
    }
}
```

Here, we test:

Multiplication with `testMultiply()`.

Division with `testDivide()`.

Handling division by zero with `testDivideByZero()`, using `assertThrows()` to check that an exception is thrown.

3. Integration Testing

While unit tests are for testing individual components, **integration tests** are used to verify how different components of a system interact. This type of testing ensures that the system functions correctly as a whole.

Example: Testing a Database Connection Here is an example of testing a method that interacts with a database:

java

```java
public class DatabaseService {
    public String getUserName(int userId) {
        // Logic to fetch the user from the database
        return "John Doe"; // Simulated database response
    }
}
```

A simple integration test might look like this:

```java

import org.junit.jupiter.api.Test;
import                                          static
org.junit.jupiter.api.Assertions.*;

public class DatabaseServiceTest {

    @Test
    public void testGetUserName() {
        DatabaseService    dbService    =    new
DatabaseService();
        String           userName          =
dbService.getUserName(1);
        assertEquals("John Doe", userName);
    }
}
```

In this case, we are testing the integration of the
DatabaseService class with the simulated database interaction.
In real-world applications, you may use **mocking** or **test
databases** to test integrations more effectively.

Mocking and Test-Driven Development (TDD)

Mocking:

In unit testing, mocking is the practice of simulating external
dependencies of the class under test. This allows you to isolate the

component being tested and avoid dependencies on databases, web services, or other external systems.

In Java, you can use **Mockito**, a popular library for mocking objects in unit tests.

Example: Using Mockito to Mock a Service:

java

```
import org.junit.jupiter.api.Test;
import static org.mockito.Mockito.*;
import                                    static
org.junit.jupiter.api.Assertions.*;

public class UserServiceTest {

    @Test
    public void testGetUserName() {
        // Mock the DatabaseService
        DatabaseService      mockDbService      =
mock(DatabaseService.class);

when(mockDbService.getUserName(1)).thenReturn("
Mocked User");

        UserService    userService    =    new
UserService(mockDbService);
```

```
    String              userName              =
userService.getUserName(1);
        assertEquals("Mocked User", userName);
    }
}
```

In this example:

- We **mock** the `DatabaseService` to return a predefined value (`"Mocked User"`) without actually accessing a real database.

- We test the `UserService` class by using the mock `DatabaseService`.

Test-Driven Development (TDD):

TDD is a development practice where you write tests before writing the actual implementation code. The basic cycle of TDD is:

Write a test for a small piece of functionality.

Run the test, and watch it fail (because the functionality isn't implemented yet).

Write the minimal code to make the test pass.

281

Refactor the code to improve its design, keeping the test passing.

This cycle helps ensure that the code is thoroughly tested and that design decisions are guided by the tests.

Real-World Example: Writing Test Cases for a User Authentication System

Let's build a simple **user authentication system** and write unit tests for it. This system will have methods to **register a user**, **login**, and **validate credentials**.

User Authentication System:
java

```java
public class AuthenticationService {

    private Map<String, String> users = new HashMap<>();  // Simulated user database

    public boolean register(String username, String password) {
        if (users.containsKey(username)) {
            return false;  // User already exists
        }
        users.put(username, password);
        return true;
```

```
    }

    public boolean login(String username, String
password) {
        return
password.equals(users.get(username));   // Check
if password matches
    }
}
```

Unit Tests for AuthenticationService:

java

```
import org.junit.jupiter.api.Test;
import                                  static
org.junit.jupiter.api.Assertions.*;

public class AuthenticationServiceTest {

    @Test
    public void testRegisterUser() {
        AuthenticationService authService = new
AuthenticationService();

assertTrue(authService.register("user1",
"password123"));

assertFalse(authService.register("user1",
"newPassword123"));   // User already exists
    }
```

```
@Test
public void testLogin() {
    AuthenticationService authService = new
AuthenticationService();
    authService.register("user1",
"password123");
    assertTrue(authService.login("user1",
"password123"));
    assertFalse(authService.login("user1",
"wrongPassword"));
    }
}
```

Explanation:

testRegisterUser() checks if the registration logic works, including checking for duplicate users.

testLogin() verifies the login functionality, ensuring that correct credentials result in a successful login and incorrect credentials result in failure.

Conclusion

In this chapter, we covered:

- **JUnit**: Writing unit tests to verify the correctness of Java methods, classes, and components.

- **Test-Driven Development (TDD)**: A methodology where tests guide the development of the code.

- **Mocking**: Using **Mockito** to simulate external dependencies and isolate the code being tested.

- **Writing unit tests for a real-world system**: We wrote tests for a simple **user authentication system** to demonstrate how to test business logic effectively.

Unit testing is an essential skill for any developer and is a cornerstone of modern software development practices. In the next chapter, we will explore **Java Streams** and how to process data in a more declarative and functional way.

CHAPTER 21

JAVA SECURITY

In this chapter, we will explore essential **Java security** concepts and how to implement them in your Java applications. Security is critical in modern applications, especially when dealing with sensitive data like passwords, financial information, and personal details. Java provides several features to ensure the integrity, confidentiality, and authentication of data and users. We will cover **cryptography**, **secure communication using SSL/TLS**, and the **Java Security Manager**. Finally, we will implement a **real-world example**: building a **secure login system** with **password hashing**.

Introduction to Cryptography in Java

Cryptography is the practice of protecting information by transforming it into an unreadable format. In Java, cryptographic operations such as encryption, decryption, hashing, and digital signatures are provided by the **Java Cryptography Architecture (JCA)**.

286

Key Cryptography Concepts:

Symmetric Encryption: The same key is used for both encryption and decryption (e.g., AES).

Asymmetric Encryption: A public key is used to encrypt data, and a private key is used to decrypt it (e.g., RSA).

Hashing: A one-way function that converts data into a fixed-length value (e.g., SHA-256, MD5). Hashing is commonly used for storing passwords securely.

Digital Signatures: Ensure the authenticity and integrity of data. A private key is used to sign data, and the corresponding public key is used to verify the signature.

Using Java's Cryptography API

Java provides the `javax.crypto` package for encryption and decryption, and `java.security` for key management and signature operations.

Example: Hashing a Password Using SHA-256

```java

import java.security.MessageDigest;
import java.security.NoSuchAlgorithmException;
```

```
public class CryptographyExample {
    public static void main(String[] args) {
        try {
            String          password          =
"securePassword123";

            // Create a MessageDigest instance
for SHA-256
            MessageDigest       digest        =
MessageDigest.getInstance("SHA-256");

            // Hash the password
            byte[]            hashBytes        =
digest.digest(password.getBytes());

            // Convert the hash to hexadecimal
format
            StringBuilder    hexString    =    new
StringBuilder();
            for (byte b : hashBytes) {

hexString.append(String.format("%02x", b));
            }

            System.out.println("Hashed password:
" + hexString.toString());

        } catch (NoSuchAlgorithmException e) {
            e.printStackTrace();
```

```
        }
    }
}
```

Explanation:

We use `MessageDigest.getInstance("SHA-256")` to get an instance of SHA-256.

The `digest()` method processes the input (the password) and returns the hashed byte array.

We then convert the byte array to a hexadecimal string for easier storage and comparison.

Secure Communication Using SSL/TLS

Secure communication over a network is crucial to protect data from eavesdropping, tampering, and forgery. **SSL (Secure Sockets Layer)** and its successor, **TLS (Transport Layer Security)**, are cryptographic protocols designed to provide secure communication over a computer network.

In Java, SSL/TLS communication is handled via the **Java Secure Socket Extension (JSSE)**. JSSE provides support for SSL/TLS protocols, allowing developers to create secure server-client communication channels.

289

Setting Up SSL/TLS in Java

You can set up SSL/TLS in Java by using the `SSLSocket` and `SSLServerSocket` classes.

Example: Secure Client-Server Communication Using SSL

SSL Server:
java

```
import javax.net.ssl.*;
import java.io.*;
import java.security.*;

public class SSLServer {
    public static void main(String[] args) {
        try {
            // Create SSL context
            SSLContext        sslContext        =
SSLContext.getInstance("TLS");
            KeyManagerFactory        kmf        =
KeyManagerFactory.getInstance(KeyManagerFactory
.getDefaultAlgorithm());
            kmf.init(getKeyStore(),
"password".toCharArray());

sslContext.init(kmf.getKeyManagers(),        null,
null);
```

```java
        // Create SSL server socket
        SSLServerSocketFactory
serverSocketFactory                    =
sslContext.getServerSocketFactory();
        SSLServerSocket    serverSocket   =
(SSLServerSocket)
serverSocketFactory.createServerSocket(1234);

        System.out.println("Secure     server
started on port 1234...");

        while (true) {
            // Accept client connections
            SSLSocket   socket  =  (SSLSocket)
serverSocket.accept();
            BufferedReader    in    =    new
BufferedReader(new
InputStreamReader(socket.getInputStream()));
            String      clientMessage     =
in.readLine();
            System.out.println("Client says:
" + clientMessage);
            socket.close();
        }
    } catch (Exception e) {
        e.printStackTrace();
    }
}
```

```java
    private static KeyStore getKeyStore() throws
Exception {
        KeyStore            keyStore            =
KeyStore.getInstance("JKS");
        FileInputStream    keyStoreFile    =    new
FileInputStream("keystore.jks");
        keyStore.load(keyStoreFile,
"password".toCharArray());
        return keyStore;
    }
}
```

SSL Client:

java

```java
import javax.net.ssl.*;
import java.io.*;

public class SSLClient {
    public static void main(String[] args) {
        try {
            // Create SSL context
            SSLContext          sslContext          =
SSLContext.getInstance("TLS");
            sslContext.init(null, null, null);

            // Create SSL socket
            SSLSocketFactory    socketFactory    =
sslContext.getSocketFactory();
```

```
        SSLSocket    socket    =    (SSLSocket)
socketFactory.createSocket("localhost", 1234);


        // Send message to server
        PrintWriter      out      =      new
PrintWriter(socket.getOutputStream(), true);
        out.println("Hello Secure Server!");
        socket.close();
    } catch (Exception e) {
        e.printStackTrace();
    }
  }
}
```

Explanation:

The **SSLServer** listens on port 1234 and accepts encrypted connections from the **SSLClient**.

The SSLContext is used to configure the secure connection.

The server uses a **keystore** (a file containing the server's private key and certificate) for authentication and encryption.

The **SSLClient** connects to the server using SSL/TLS and sends an encrypted message.

Understanding Java's Security Manager and Permissions

Java's **Security Manager** is used to control access to system resources such as files, network sockets, and other sensitive operations. The Security Manager enforces security policies defined by the **policy file**, which specifies what actions are allowed or denied for specific classes.

Setting Up a Security Manager

You can set up a **SecurityManager** by calling `System.setSecurityManager()` at the start of your application.

java

```
public class SecurityManagerExample {
    public static void main(String[] args) {
        System.setSecurityManager(new
SecurityManager());
        try {
            // Trying to access a sensitive
operation (e.g., file reading)
            File         file      =       new
File("importantFile.txt");
            FileReader       fr      =       new
FileReader(file);
            System.out.println("File       read
successfully.");
```

```
        } catch (SecurityException e) {

System.out.println("SecurityException:    Access
denied");
        } catch (IOException e) {
            e.printStackTrace();
        }
    }
}
```

Explanation:

> The `SecurityManager` is set up to prevent unauthorized access.

> If the operation violates the security policy, a `SecurityException` is thrown.

> In the example, trying to access a file without the appropriate permission would result in a `SecurityException`.

Policy File:

You can define security policies in a policy file, which specifies permissions for Java code. A sample policy file might look like this:

plaintext

```
grant {
    permission          java.io.FilePermission
"/path/to/file", "read";
};
```

This policy allows reading files from /path/to/file.

Real-World Example: Building a Secure Login System with Password Hashing

Now, let's build a **secure login system** where user passwords are stored securely using **hashing**. In real-world applications, passwords should never be stored in plaintext. Instead, you should use a cryptographic hash function like **SHA-256** to store a hashed version of the password.

User Authentication System with Password Hashing:
java

```
import java.security.*;
import java.util.Base64;


public class AuthenticationService {

    private    static    final    String    SALT    =
"somesalt";
```

```java
    public static String hashPassword(String
password) {
        try {
            MessageDigest digest =
MessageDigest.getInstance("SHA-256");
            String saltedPassword = password +
SALT;
            byte[] hashBytes =
digest.digest(saltedPassword.getBytes());
            return
Base64.getEncoder().encodeToString(hashBytes);
        } catch (NoSuchAlgorithmException e) {
            throw new RuntimeException("Error
hashing password", e);
        }
    }

    public static boolean
validatePassword(String inputPassword, String
storedPasswordHash) {
        String inputPasswordHash =
hashPassword(inputPassword);
        return
inputPasswordHash.equals(storedPasswordHash);
    }

    public static void main(String[] args) {
        String password = "securePassword123";
```

297

```
        String          storedPasswordHash    =
hashPassword(password);

        // User attempts to log in with a
password
        String          inputPassword         =
"securePassword123";
        if      (validatePassword(inputPassword,
storedPasswordHash)) {
            System.out.println("Login
successful!");
        } else {
            System.out.println("Invalid
password.");
        }
    }
}
```

Explanation:

The hashPassword() method uses **SHA-256** to hash the password, with an added **salt** for added security.

The validatePassword() method compares the hash of the input password with the stored hash to authenticate the user.

Base64 encoding is used to convert the byte array into a readable string that can be stored in a database.

298

Output:

```
nginx
```

```
Login successful!
```

This example demonstrates how to hash and validate passwords securely, which is essential for protecting user data in real-world applications.

Conclusion

In this chapter, we explored **Java security** concepts, including:

Cryptography in Java, including encryption, decryption, and password hashing.

SSL/TLS communication for secure data exchange between clients and servers.

Java Security Manager to enforce security policies and restrict unauthorized access to system resources.

A **real-world example** of building a **secure login system** using password hashing for user authentication.

Java offers a wide range of tools and APIs to ensure that your applications are secure. In the next chapter, we will explore **Java Networking** in more detail and learn how to build networked applications. Let's continue enhancing our Java skills!

CHAPTER 22

DESIGN PATTERNS IN JAVA

In this chapter, we will explore **design patterns** in Java—reusable solutions to common software design problems. Design patterns represent best practices that can be applied to solve complex problems in a way that is both efficient and maintainable. We will cover several common design patterns, including the **Singleton**, **Factory**, and **Observer** patterns, and discuss their benefits and real-world applications. We will also implement a **real-world example** by applying the **Singleton pattern** to create a global logger class.

Introduction to Design Patterns

A **design pattern** is a general reusable solution to a commonly occurring problem in software design. It is not a finished design but rather a template or description for solving a particular problem in various contexts. Design patterns are generally classified into three categories:

Creational Patterns: Deal with object creation mechanisms. Examples include **Singleton**, **Factory Method**, and **Abstract Factory**.

Structural Patterns: Concerned with how classes and objects are composed to form larger structures. Examples include **Adapter**, **Composite**, and **Facade**.

Behavioral Patterns: Deal with communication between objects and the responsibilities of objects. Examples include **Observer**, **Strategy**, and **Command**.

Using design patterns promotes code reusability, maintainability, and scalability. They also help developers communicate effectively, as design patterns provide a common vocabulary.

Benefits of Using Design Patterns in Java Programming

Reusability: Design patterns provide proven solutions to common problems, so you don't need to reinvent the wheel.

Scalability: Design patterns help you write code that is scalable and adaptable to change.

Maintainability: Design patterns promote clean and organized code, making it easier to maintain and extend.

Separation of Concerns: Patterns help separate the different aspects of an application, reducing complexity and improving clarity.

Communication: Patterns provide a common vocabulary that allows developers to discuss solutions more effectively.

Common Design Patterns in Java

Let's take a look at some of the most widely used design patterns in Java:

1. Singleton Pattern

The **Singleton pattern** ensures that a class has only one instance and provides a global point of access to that instance. This pattern is typically used when a single instance of a class is required to control access to resources, such as a global logger, database connection, or configuration manager.

Key Concept: Restrict the instantiation of a class to one object.

Use Case: Logging, database connections, thread pools.

2. Factory Pattern

The **Factory pattern** is a creational pattern that provides an interface for creating objects in a super class but allows subclasses to alter the type of objects that will be created.

Key Concept: Define an interface for creating objects but let subclasses decide which class to instantiate.

Use Case: Creating objects without specifying the exact class to be created (e.g., GUI component creation).

3. Observer Pattern

The **Observer pattern** is a behavioral design pattern where an object (subject) maintains a list of dependents (observers) that need to be notified of any state changes in the subject.

Key Concept: Maintain a one-to-many dependency between objects so that when one object changes state, all its dependents are notified and updated automatically.

Use Case: Event handling systems, UI frameworks, and messaging systems.

Real-World Example: Implementing the Singleton Pattern to Create a Global Logger Class

The **Singleton pattern** is perfect for creating a **global logger** that ensures only one instance of the logger class is used throughout the application. This prevents multiple instances of the logger, which could cause inconsistent log messages.

Step 1: Define the Singleton Logger Class

We will create a `Logger` class that follows the Singleton pattern. This class will have a `log` method that writes log messages to the console.

```java
public class Logger {

    // The private static instance of the Logger class
    private static Logger instance;

    // Private constructor to prevent instantiation from outside
    private Logger() {}

    // Public method to get the instance of the Logger class
    public static Logger getInstance() {
        if (instance == null) {
            // Create the instance only when it's needed (Lazy initialization)
            instance = new Logger();
        }
        return instance;
    }
```

```
    // Method to log messages
    public void log(String message) {
        System.out.println("Log    Message:    "    +
message);
    }
}
```

Explanation:

  Private Constructor: The constructor is private to prevent instantiation from outside the class.

  Static Instance: The `instance` variable holds the single instance of the class. It is initialized only when needed (lazy initialization).

  Thread-Safety: In a multithreaded environment, you might want to make the `getInstance()` method thread-safe. For simplicity, we're using a basic implementation, but in a production system, we could use **synchronized blocks** or **double-checked locking** to ensure thread-safety.

Step 2: Using the Logger Singleton

To demonstrate the use of the Singleton pattern, let's use the `Logger` class in a sample program.

java

```java
public class Application {

    public static void main(String[] args) {
        // Get the singleton instance of the
Logger class
        Logger logger1 = Logger.getInstance();
        logger1.log("This is the first log
message.");

        // Try to get another instance of the
Logger (it should be the same instance)
        Logger logger2 = Logger.getInstance();
        logger2.log("This is the second log
message.");

        // Check if both instances are the same
        System.out.println("Are both logger
instances the same? " + (logger1 == logger2));
    }
}
```

Explanation:

We retrieve the singleton instance of the `Logger` class by calling `Logger.getInstance()`.

We log two messages using the `log()` method. Since we are using the Singleton pattern, both `logger1` and `logger2` refer to the same instance.

The output of the == comparison will confirm that both references point to the same object.

Output:

```
pgsql

Log Message: This is the first log message.
Log Message: This is the second log message.
Are both logger instances the same? true
```

Conclusion

In this chapter, we covered:

Design Patterns: Reusable solutions to common software design problems.

Singleton Pattern: Ensuring only one instance of a class, commonly used for logging, configuration management, etc.

Factory Pattern and **Observer Pattern**: Additional examples of design patterns that help in object creation and managing state changes, respectively.

Real-World Example: Implementing the **Singleton pattern** to create a global logger that can be accessed throughout an application.

Design patterns are essential tools for software developers, allowing them to write clean, maintainable, and reusable code. In the next chapter, we will explore **Java Networking** in more detail and learn how to build networked applications. Let's continue enhancing our Java expertise!

CHAPTER 23

JAVA 8 AND BEYOND: NEW FEATURES

In this chapter, we will explore the significant enhancements introduced in **Java 8** and beyond, focusing on features like **default methods in interfaces**, the **Optional** class, **method references**, and the new **Stream API**. These features have transformed the way Java developers write code by enabling more concise, functional, and expressive programming. By the end of this chapter, we will refactor an existing codebase using Java 8 features such as **Streams** and **Lambdas** to demonstrate how these concepts can improve readability and efficiency.

Introduction to New Features in Java 8 and Beyond

Java 8 was a landmark release in the Java ecosystem, introducing several major features that significantly enhance the language's expressiveness and functionality. These features include:

Lambda Expressions: Allow you to write concise, functional code by treating functionality as arguments.

Streams API: Provides a new abstraction for processing sequences of elements (e.g., collections) in a functional style.

Default Methods in Interfaces: Enables interfaces to have methods with default implementations, solving the problem of adding new methods to interfaces without breaking existing implementations.

Optional Class: Represents a value that may or may not be present, helping to avoid **NullPointerExceptions**.

Method References: A shorthand notation for invoking methods using the : : operator.

In later versions of Java (Java 9 and beyond), new features were added, such as **Modules**, **Private methods in interfaces**, **JVM improvements**, and **Pattern matching** (in progress). However, Java 8 remains the most transformative release in terms of language features.

Default Methods in Interfaces

Before Java 8, interfaces could only declare method signatures, leaving the actual implementation to the implementing class. This caused problems when developers needed to add new methods to existing interfaces—doing so would break backward compatibility.

Java 8 introduced **default methods**, allowing interfaces to provide concrete methods with default implementations. This allows you to add new methods to interfaces without affecting existing classes that implement those interfaces.

Example: Default Method in Interface

java

```java
interface MyInterface {
    // Abstract method
    void abstractMethod();

    // Default method
    default void defaultMethod() {
        System.out.println("This is a default
method in the interface.");
    }
}

class MyClass implements MyInterface {
    public void abstractMethod() {
        System.out.println("Implementation    of
abstract method.");
    }
}
```

```
public class DefaultMethodExample {
    public static void main(String[] args) {
        MyClass myClass = new MyClass();
        myClass.abstractMethod();
        myClass.defaultMethod();  // Calling the
default method
    }
}
```

Explanation:

> `MyInterface` declares a default method `defaultMethod()`.

The class `MyClass` implements the `MyInterface` and provides an implementation for `abstractMethod()`.

`defaultMethod()` is inherited automatically, and the class does not need to implement it unless desired.

Output:

```
csharp
```

```
Implementation of abstract method.
This is a default method in the interface.
```

The Optional Class

Java 8 introduced the **Optional** class, which is used to represent a value that may or may not be present. It helps avoid NullPointerException by explicitly indicating the presence or absence of a value. Instead of returning null to indicate a missing value, you can return an Optional that contains a value or is empty.

Example: Using the Optional Class

java

```
import java.util.Optional;

public class OptionalExample {
    public static void main(String[] args) {
        String name = null;

        // Using Optional to safely handle null
values
        Optional<String>       optionalName      =
Optional.ofNullable(name);

        // If a value is present, print it;
otherwise, print a default message
        String                result            =
optionalName.orElse("Name not provided");
        System.out.println(result);  // Output:
Name not provided
```

```
    }
}
```

Explanation:

We use `Optional.ofNullable()` to wrap the `name` variable, which may be `null`.

The `orElse()` method provides a default value ("Name not provided") when the `Optional` is empty (i.e., the value is `null`).

Output:

```
nginx
```

```
Name not provided
```

`Optional` can also be used to perform actions like filtering, mapping, and checking if a value is present.

Method References

Method references in Java 8 provide a shorthand notation for invoking methods. A method reference is a concise and readable way of referring to methods without invoking them. This is especially useful when using functional interfaces (e.g., with **Streams** or **Lambdas**).

315

There are four types of method references:

Reference to a static method

Reference to an instance method of a specific object

Reference to an instance method of an arbitrary object of a particular type

Reference to a constructor

Example: Using Method References
java

```java
import java.util.Arrays;
import java.util.List;

public class MethodReferenceExample {
    public static void main(String[] args) {
        List<String>          names          =
Arrays.asList("Alice", "Bob", "Charlie");

        // Using method reference to print each
name
        names.forEach(System.out::println);   //
Equivalent    to:    names.forEach(name    ->
System.out.println(name));
    }
}
```

Explanation:

> `System.out::println` is à method reference that refers to the `println()` method of `System.out`.

> It is equivalent to using a lambda expression `name -> System.out.println(name)`, but the method reference is more concise.

Output:

```
nginx

Alice
Bob
Charlie
```

Real-World Example: Refactoring Codebase with Streams and Lambdas

Now, let's refactor an existing codebase to leverage Java 8 **Streams** and **Lambdas** for better readability and performance.

Old Way: Iterating Over a List

Before Java 8, iterating over a collection (e.g., a `List`) was typically done using a `for` loop.

```
java

import java.util.ArrayList;
import java.util.List;

public class OldWayExample {
    public static void main(String[] args) {
        List<String> names = new ArrayList<>();
        names.add("Alice");
        names.add("Bob");
        names.add("Charlie");

        // Old way: Using for loop
        for (String name : names) {
            if (name.startsWith("A")) {
                System.out.println(name);
            }
        }
    }
}
```

Explanation:

We iterate over the list using a for loop and check if each name starts with the letter "A". If it does, we print the name.

Output:

```
nginx
```

Alice

Refactored Code: Using Streams and Lambdas

With Java 8, we can replace the `for` loop with **Streams** and **Lambdas** to make the code more concise and expressive.

java

```java
import java.util.ArrayList;
import java.util.List;

public class NewWayExample {
    public static void main(String[] args) {
        List<String> names = new ArrayList<>();
        names.add("Alice");
        names.add("Bob");
        names.add("Charlie");

        // New way: Using Streams and Lambdas
        names.stream()
            .filter(name                    ->
name.startsWith("A"))
            .forEach(System.out::println);   //
Equivalent    to:     names.forEach(name    ->
System.out.println(name));
    }
}
```

Explanation:

`names.stream()` creates a stream from the list of names.

`.filter(name -> name.startsWith("A"))` filters the names that start with the letter "A".

`.forEach(System.out::println)` prints each filtered name.

Output:

`nginx`

`Alice`

Advantages of Refactoring:

The code is more concise and readable.

The use of **Streams** allows us to express the entire pipeline of operations in a declarative manner.

We avoided the manual iteration and conditional logic, letting the **Stream API** handle the flow.

Conclusion

In this chapter, we covered:

Java 8 Features: Introduction to significant changes like **Lambdas, Streams, default methods in interfaces, Optional**, and **method references**.

Refactoring Code: How Java 8 features help you write cleaner, more efficient, and maintainable code.

Real-World Example: Refactoring an existing codebase to use **Streams** and **Lambdas** for more concise and functional code.

The features introduced in Java 8 significantly changed the way Java developers write code. By embracing **functional programming paradigms** and utilizing **Streams** and **Lambdas**, you can make your Java applications more readable, concise, and efficient. In the next chapter, we will explore **Java Modules** introduced in Java 9 to manage dependencies and modularize applications. Let's continue enhancing our Java skills!

CHAPTER 24

JAVA VIRTUAL MACHINE (JVM) AND MEMORY MANAGEMENT

In this chapter, we will dive deep into the **Java Virtual Machine (JVM)** and its role in running Java applications. We will explore how the JVM handles **memory management**, the concept of **garbage collection**, and the different techniques used for **optimizing memory usage**. Additionally, we will discuss profiling and debugging tools like **JVisualVM** to analyze and improve the performance of Java applications.

Understanding the JVM and Garbage Collection

The **Java Virtual Machine (JVM)** is the engine that drives Java applications. It takes the compiled bytecode of a Java program and executes it on a specific hardware platform. The JVM performs several critical tasks, including memory management, garbage collection, and execution of Java bytecode.

JVM Architecture

The JVM consists of several components that work together to execute Java programs:

Class Loader: Loads classes into memory.

Runtime Data Areas: Includes the **heap, stack, method area, program counter (PC)**, and **native method stacks**.

Execution Engine: Executes the bytecode in a thread.

Garbage Collector (GC): Automatically manages memory by reclaiming unused memory objects.

Garbage Collection in Java

Garbage Collection (GC) is the process of automatically identifying and removing unused objects from memory, thus preventing memory leaks. In Java, the garbage collector runs in the background, freeing up memory that is no longer referenced by the program. The JVM uses different types of garbage collection algorithms, such as **serial garbage collection, parallel garbage collection, CMS (Concurrent Mark-Sweep)**, and **G1 garbage collection**.

The process of garbage collection involves:

Marking: Identifying which objects are still in use (reachable objects).

Sweeping: Removing objects that are no longer referenced.

Compacting: Reorganizing memory to reduce fragmentation.

323

Garbage Collection Example

Java automatically handles memory allocation and garbage collection. Here's a simple example to demonstrate this:

java

```java
public class GarbageCollectionExample {
    public static void main(String[] args) {
        // Creating objects
        String str1 = new String("Hello");
        String str2 = new String("World");

        // Assign null to one object, making it eligible for garbage collection
        str1 = null;

        // Suggest garbage collection
        System.gc();        // Calling garbage collector (Note: This is just a suggestion)
    }

    @Override
    protected void finalize() throws Throwable {
        super.finalize();
        System.out.println("Object is being garbage collected.");
    }
}
```

Explanation:

The `str1` object is set to `null`, making it eligible for garbage collection.

The `System.gc()` method is a suggestion to the JVM to perform garbage collection (the JVM may or may not execute it at that moment).

The `finalize()` method is called just before an object is garbage collected, allowing cleanup before the object is removed.

Note: `finalize()` is deprecated in recent versions of Java, and developers are encouraged to use `try-with-resources` or other mechanisms for resource management.

Memory Management and Optimization in Java

Java's memory management is divided into several parts, each with specific responsibilities to ensure the program runs efficiently.

Memory Areas in the JVM

Heap: This is where objects are stored. The heap is divided into:

Young Generation: Newly created objects, where most of the garbage collection occurs.

Old Generation: Long-lived objects that survive multiple garbage collection cycles.

Permanent Generation (removed in Java 8 and replaced with Metaspace): Stores class definitions and metadata.

Stack: Each thread has its own stack, which stores method calls, local variables, and return addresses. The stack is used to manage method invocations.

Method Area (Metaspace): Stores metadata about the classes being used by the JVM, such as field and method data. Starting with Java 8, Metaspace replaces the older Permanent Generation.

Optimizing Memory Management

Effective memory management involves reducing memory usage, optimizing garbage collection, and managing the heap to avoid memory leaks. Here are some optimization tips:

Use Object Pools: Reuse objects rather than creating new instances repeatedly. This is especially useful for expensive objects like database connections or threads.

326

Avoid Memory Leaks: Ensure that objects are dereferenced when no longer needed. The garbage collector cannot reclaim objects that are still referenced.

Minimize Object Creation: Excessive object creation can lead to frequent garbage collection. Try to minimize the creation of short-lived objects.

Tune JVM Garbage Collection: Depending on your application's requirements, you can fine-tune the garbage collection process by choosing the appropriate GC algorithm and adjusting heap sizes.

Example of Tuning Garbage Collection Parameters

You can adjust garbage collection behavior using JVM options:

```bash
java   -XX:+UseG1GC   -Xms512m   -Xmx1024m
MyApplication
```

Explanation:

-XX:+UseG1GC: Enables the **G1 Garbage Collector**, which is optimal for applications that handle large heaps.

-Xms512m: Sets the initial heap size to 512 MB.

327

-Xmx1024m: Sets the maximum heap size to 1024 MB.

Profiling and Debugging Java Applications

Profiling and debugging are essential to identify performance bottlenecks, memory leaks, and other issues in Java applications. Several tools are available for profiling and debugging Java applications.

1. JVisualVM

JVisualVM is a powerful tool bundled with the JDK that allows you to monitor, profile, and troubleshoot Java applications. You can use JVisualVM to inspect memory usage, garbage collection activity, CPU usage, and thread behavior in real-time.

Key Features of JVisualVM:

> **Heap Dump**: Capture and analyze the memory heap to identify objects consuming memory.

> **Garbage Collection Monitoring**: Track garbage collection activities and determine how often the GC runs.

> **CPU Profiling**: Analyze which methods are consuming the most CPU time.

Example: Analyzing a Java Application with JVisualVM

Start Your Application: Run your Java application in the usual way:

```bash
```

```
java -jar MyApplication.jar
```

Launch JVisualVM: Open JVisualVM by running the following command (in JDK 8, it's typically located in the `bin` folder):

```bash
```

```
jvisualvm
```

Attach JVisualVM to Your Application: In the JVisualVM interface, your running application will appear in the left panel under **Local** or **Remote** (if it's running remotely). Double-click your application to start monitoring.

Monitor Memory Usage: Go to the **Monitor** tab to view memory usage in real-time. JVisualVM will show you the heap size and garbage collection activity. If you notice high memory usage or frequent GC events, you may want to investigate further using the **Heap Dump** or **Profiler** tools.

329

Analyze Heap Dumps: If you suspect a memory leak, capture a **heap dump** and analyze the objects that are using the most memory.

CPU Profiling: Go to the **Profiler** tab to start profiling CPU usage. This will show you the methods that consume the most CPU time, helping you pinpoint performance bottlenecks.

Real-World Example: Analyzing the Performance of a Java Application Using Tools like JVisualVM

Let's say you have a Java application that processes large datasets, and you are experiencing performance issues, such as high memory usage or slow execution. To diagnose the problem, you can use **JVisualVM**:

Start the Application: Run your application as usual.

Attach JVisualVM: Open JVisualVM and attach it to your running application.

Monitor Memory Usage: In the **Monitor** tab, observe the memory usage. You may notice frequent garbage collection events, which indicate that your application is creating and discarding a large number of objects.

Take a Heap Dump: If memory usage is high, take a heap dump to inspect which objects are consuming the most memory. You may find that large collections or caches are not being cleared properly, leading to excessive memory consumption.

Profile CPU Usage: Go to the **Profiler** tab and start profiling CPU usage. You might discover that certain methods take a long time to execute, indicating performance bottlenecks.

Optimize Based on Findings: Based on the analysis, you might decide to optimize memory usage by reducing object creation, using caching, or adjusting garbage collection parameters.

Conclusion

In this chapter, we:

Explored the **Java Virtual Machine (JVM)** and its role in running Java applications, with a focus on **garbage collection** and **memory management**.

Learned how to optimize memory usage by tuning garbage collection, managing heap sizes, and avoiding memory leaks.

Discussed **profiling and debugging** tools like **JVisualVM** for monitoring and analyzing Java application performance.

Provided a **real-world example** of using JVisualVM to analyze and improve the performance of a Java application.

Memory management and performance optimization are critical for building scalable and efficient Java applications. In the next chapter, we will dive into **Java Modules** and how they help with modularization and managing dependencies in large applications.

CHAPTER 25

BUILDING WEB APPLICATIONS WITH JAVA

In this chapter, we will explore the fundamentals of **building web applications with Java**. We'll cover the essential technologies and tools that are commonly used for creating web applications, including **servlets**, **JSP (JavaServer Pages)**, and web frameworks like **Spring**. We will also delve into the **request-response lifecycle** in web applications and how to build **RESTful APIs** with Java. By the end of this chapter, you will be able to develop a **simple blog application** using **Java servlets** and **JSP**.

Introduction to Servlets, JSP, and Web Application Frameworks like Spring

Java provides a robust set of tools for building web applications, starting with **servlets** and **JavaServer Pages (JSP)**. These technologies enable you to handle HTTP requests and responses, create dynamic web pages, and build server-side logic.

333

1. Servlets

A **servlet** is a Java class that handles HTTP requests and generates responses. Servlets are part of the Java EE (Enterprise Edition) standard and form the core of most Java-based web applications. They can process form data, handle session management, interact with databases, and perform other backend tasks.

A typical **Servlet** performs the following functions:

Receive HTTP requests from clients (e.g., web browsers).

Process requests by interacting with backend resources, such as databases or other services.

Generate HTTP responses to send back to the client.

2. JavaServer Pages (JSP)

JSP allows developers to create dynamic web pages using HTML, XML, or other document types, embedded with Java code. While servlets provide a way to generate dynamic content, JSP makes it easier to embed Java logic directly into HTML pages using special tags.

3. Spring Framework

Spring is a comprehensive framework for building Java-based web applications. It provides a wide range of capabilities, including:

Spring MVC: A Model-View-Controller framework for building web applications.

Spring Boot: Simplifies the process of setting up and configuring Spring-based applications.

Spring Data: Provides easy integration with databases using JPA or other data sources.

Spring is widely used for building enterprise-level applications due to its modular and flexible architecture.

Request-Response Lifecycle in Web Applications

Understanding the **request-response lifecycle** is crucial for building efficient and scalable web applications. The lifecycle consists of several stages:

Client Makes a Request: A client (typically a web browser) sends an HTTP request to the server. This request can be for a static resource (e.g., an image or an HTML file) or for dynamic content generated by a servlet or JSP.

Server Receives the Request: The web server (e.g., Apache Tomcat) receives the HTTP request and forwards it to the appropriate servlet or JSP based on the URL pattern.

Servlet/JSP Processes the Request: The servlet or JSP handles the request, performs any necessary business logic, interacts with databases, and prepares the data to be returned.

Server Sends a Response: After processing, the servlet or JSP generates an HTTP response, which could be HTML, JSON, XML, or any other content type. This response is sent back to the client.

Client Receives the Response: The client receives the response from the server, which could be rendered as a web page, displayed as JSON data, or used in another way.

Building RESTful APIs with Java

A **RESTful API** is a web service that adheres to the principles of **Representational State Transfer (REST)**. REST APIs are stateless, scalable, and commonly used for creating web services in Java applications. They use standard HTTP methods such as **GET**, **POST**, **PUT**, and **DELETE** to perform operations on resources.

Creating a Simple RESTful API in Java

We can build a simple RESTful API using **JAX-RS (Java API for RESTful Web Services)** or by using the **Spring framework**, which simplifies the development of RESTful services.

Example: Building a Simple RESTful API with JAX-RS

```java
import javax.ws.rs.*;
import javax.ws.rs.core.MediaType;
import javax.ws.rs.core.Response;

@Path("/api")
public class BlogAPI {

    @GET
    @Path("/post/{id}")
    @Produces(MediaType.APPLICATION_JSON)
    public Response getPost(@PathParam("id") int id) {
        // Simulate retrieving a blog post from a database
```

```java
        BlogPost post = new BlogPost(id, "Sample
Blog Post", "This is a sample post.");

        return Response.ok(post).build();
    }


    @POST
    @Path("/post")
    @Consumes(MediaType.APPLICATION_JSON)
    public Response createPost(BlogPost post) {
        // Simulate saving the blog post to a
database
        System.out.println("Created blog post: "
+ post);
        return
Response.status(Response.Status.CREATED).entity
(post).build();
    }


    // BlogPost model
    public static class BlogPost {
        private int id;
        private String title;
        private String content;

        public BlogPost() {}

        public BlogPost(int id, String title,
String content) {
```

```
            this.id = id;
            this.title = title;
            this.content = content;
        }

        // Getters and setters
        public int getId() {
            return id;
        }
        public void setId(int id) {
            this.id = id;
        }
        public String getTitle() {
            return title;
        }
        public void setTitle(String title) {
            this.title = title;
        }
        public String getContent() {
            return content;
        }
        public void setContent(String content) {
            this.content = content;
        }
    }
}
```

Explanation:

This API provides two endpoints:

GET /api/post/{id}: Retrieves a blog post by its ID.

POST /api/post: Creates a new blog post by accepting a JSON object in the request body.

We use **JAX-RS annotations** (@GET, @POST, @Path) to define the endpoints and request methods.

Real-World Example: Developing a Simple Blog Application Using Java Servlets and JSP

Let's build a **simple blog application** using **Java servlets** and **JSP**. This application will allow users to view a list of blog posts and add new posts.

Step 1: Set Up a Simple Servlet to Handle Blog Posts

java

```java
import java.io.*;
import javax.servlet.*;
import javax.servlet.http.*;
import java.util.*;

public class BlogServlet extends HttpServlet {
    private List<String> posts = new ArrayList<>();
```

```java
// Initialize with some default posts
@Override
public void init() throws ServletException {
    posts.add("First Blog Post");
    posts.add("Second Blog Post");
}


// Handle GET request: Display list of blog posts
@Override
protected void doGet(HttpServletRequest request, HttpServletResponse response)
        throws ServletException, IOException
{
    request.setAttribute("posts", posts);
    RequestDispatcher dispatcher = request.getRequestDispatcher("blog.jsp");
    dispatcher.forward(request, response);
}


// Handle POST request: Add a new blog post
@Override
protected void doPost(HttpServletRequest request, HttpServletResponse response)
        throws ServletException, IOException
{
    String newPost = request.getParameter("newPost");
```

```
        if      (newPost     !=      null      &&
!newPost.isEmpty()) {
        posts.add(newPost);
    }
    response.sendRedirect("blog");
  }
}
```

Explanation:

The `BlogServlet` handles both **GET** and **POST** requests.

GET request: Displays the list of blog posts.

POST request: Adds a new blog post.

Step 2: Create the JSP Page to Display Blog Posts

jsp

```jsp
<%@ page language="java" contentType="text/html;
charset=ISO-8859-1" pageEncoding="ISO-8859-1"%>
<!DOCTYPE html>
<html>
<head>
    <meta charset="ISO-8859-1">
    <title>Blog</title>
</head>
<body>
    <h1>Blog Posts</h1>
    <ul>
```

```
    <c:forEach var="post" items="${posts}">
        <li>${post}</li>
    </c:forEach>
  </ul>

  <h2>Add a New Post</h2>
  <form action="blog" method="POST">
      <input    type="text"    name="newPost"
placeholder="Enter new post" required>
      <input type="submit" value="Add Post">
  </form>
</body>
</html>
```

Explanation:

The JSP page receives the list of posts from the servlet and
displays them using the <c:forEach> tag.

It also includes a form to allow users to submit new blog posts.

Step 3: Configure the Web Application in web.xml

xml

```
<web-app
xmlns="http://java.sun.com/xml/ns/javaee"

xmlns:xsi="http://www.w3.org/2001/XMLSchema-
instance"
```

```
xsi:schemaLocation="http://java.sun.com/xml/ns/
javaee

http://java.sun.com/xml/ns/javaee/web-
app_3_1.xsd"
        version="3.1">

    <servlet>
        <servlet-name>BlogServlet</servlet-
name>
        <servlet-class>BlogServlet</servlet-
class>
    </servlet>

    <servlet-mapping>
        <servlet-name>BlogServlet</servlet-
name>
        <url-pattern>/blog</url-pattern>
    </servlet-mapping>

</web-app>
```

Explanation:

The `web.xml` file defines the servlet and its URL mapping (`/blog`), so when the user visits `/blog`, the `BlogServlet` will be invoked.

Conclusion

In this chapter, we:

Explored the fundamental building blocks of web applications in Java: **servlets**, **JSP**, and **Spring**.

Discussed the **request-response lifecycle** in web applications and how the server processes client requests.

Learned how to build a simple **RESTful API** using JAX-RS.

Developed a **simple blog application** using **Java servlets** and **JSP** for handling dynamic content.

Web development in Java offers powerful tools and frameworks for building scalable and secure applications. In the next chapter, we will explore **Java security** to help you protect your applications from security threats. Let's continue enhancing our Java development skills!

CHAPTER 26

ADVANCED JAVA TOPICS

In this chapter, we will explore some of the more advanced topics in Java programming, which are crucial for building high-performance applications. Specifically, we will cover **Java Virtual Machine (JVM) tuning and performance optimization**, **advanced concurrency and parallelism techniques**, and **Java's memory model** with **atomic operations**. These concepts are critical when working on applications that demand high throughput, low latency, or efficient resource management, such as trading platforms, financial systems, or large-scale enterprise applications.

Java Virtual Machine (JVM) Tuning and Performance Optimization

The **Java Virtual Machine (JVM)** is responsible for executing Java bytecode and managing resources like memory. Understanding and optimizing the performance of the JVM is crucial for building efficient, high-performance applications. JVM performance tuning involves optimizing how the JVM allocates memory, handles garbage collection, and manages threads.

Key JVM Tuning Concepts

Heap Size Management The JVM's heap is where objects are stored, and managing its size is crucial for performance. Too small a heap will result in frequent garbage collection, while too large a heap may lead to longer garbage collection pauses. JVM tuning allows you to adjust the initial and maximum heap sizes with -Xms (initial heap size) and -Xmx (maximum heap size).

Example:

```bash
```

```
java -Xms512m -Xmx2048m MyApp
```

This configuration sets the initial heap size to 512 MB and the maximum heap size to 2 GB.

Garbage Collection (GC) Tuning Java uses garbage collection to automatically reclaim memory used by objects that are no longer reachable. However, GC can introduce latency, especially in real-time applications. There are different garbage collectors (e.g., **Serial GC, Parallel GC, G1 GC**), and choosing the right one depends on the application's requirements.

Serial GC: Best for single-threaded applications with small heap sizes.

Parallel GC: Optimized for multi-threaded applications with a larger heap.

G1 GC: Designed for applications with large heaps and low-latency requirements.

Example:

bash

```
java -XX:+UseG1GC -Xms512m -Xmx2g MyApp
```

JVM JIT Compiler (Just-In-Time Compilation) The JVM uses a **JIT compiler** to improve the performance of Java applications. It compiles bytecode into native machine code at runtime, which reduces execution time for frequently executed code.

JVM Monitoring and Profiling Tools Tools like **JVisualVM, JProfiler**, and **Java Flight Recorder** are useful for profiling JVM applications and identifying performance bottlenecks such as high CPU usage, memory leaks, or inefficient garbage collection. Monitoring JVM metrics like **heap usage**, **garbage**

collection statistics, and **thread behavior** can help optimize performance.

Example: Optimizing JVM for High-Performance Trading Application

In a high-frequency trading system, minimizing latency and maximizing throughput are critical. You can tune the JVM to ensure minimal garbage collection pauses and efficient use of resources:

bash

```
java    -Xms1g    -Xmx4g    -XX:+UseG1GC    -
XX:MaxGCPauseMillis=100    -XX:ParallelGCThreads=8
MyTradingApp
```

This command sets the heap size to 1 GB and 4 GB, uses the **G1 GC**, and configures the JVM to target a maximum garbage collection pause of 100 ms with 8 parallel GC threads.

Advanced Concurrency and Parallelism Techniques

Java has powerful concurrency and parallelism capabilities, allowing developers to write multi-threaded applications that efficiently utilize available CPU cores. Advanced concurrency techniques are essential for creating responsive, scalable applications that perform well under heavy load.

1. Thread Pools and Executor Framework

Java's **Executor Framework** simplifies the management of threads, particularly when working with large numbers of threads or tasks. The **ThreadPoolExecutor** class provides a way to efficiently manage a pool of threads, which can execute tasks concurrently.

Example: Using ExecutorService

```java
import java.util.concurrent.*;

public class ExecutorServiceExample {
    public static void main(String[] args) throws
InterruptedException, ExecutionException {
        ExecutorService           executor           =
Executors.newFixedThreadPool(4);

        Callable<Integer> task = () -> {
            // Simulate a computation task
            Thread.sleep(1000);
            return 42;
        };
```

```
        Future<Integer>        future        =
executor.submit(task);
        Integer result = future.get();
        System.out.println("Task   result:   "   +
result);

        executor.shutdown();
    }
}
```

Explanation:

We create a thread pool with 4 threads using `Executors.newFixedThreadPool(4)`.

We define a task using the `Callable` interface, which can return a result.

The `submit()` method returns a `Future` object, which we can use to retrieve the result of the task once it's completed.

2. Fork/Join Framework

The **Fork/Join framework** is used for parallel processing of tasks that can be recursively split into smaller tasks. It helps with dividing a problem into multiple tasks and executing them in parallel.

Example: ForkJoinPool

java

```java
import java.util.concurrent.*;

public class ForkJoinExample {
    public static void main(String[] args) {
        ForkJoinPool    forkJoinPool    =    new
ForkJoinPool();

        // Create a task that performs a simple
parallel sum
        RecursiveTask<Integer>    task    =    new
RecursiveTask<>() {
            @Override
            protected Integer compute() {
                return 10 + 20;
            }
        };

        // Invoke the task
        Integer             result             =
forkJoinPool.invoke(task);
        System.out.println("Sum    result:    "    +
result);
    }
}
```

Explanation:

The `ForkJoinPool` is used to execute a `RecursiveTask`, which performs a parallel sum.

This framework is highly efficient for recursive tasks that can be broken down into smaller sub-tasks.

3. Parallel Streams

Java 8 introduced the **Stream API**, which allows you to process sequences of elements (like collections) in a functional style. You can convert a regular stream into a parallel stream using `.parallel()` to execute operations concurrently.

Example: Parallel Streams

```java
java

import java.util.Arrays;

public class ParallelStreamExample {
    public static void main(String[] args) {
        int[] numbers = {1, 2, 3, 4, 5, 6, 7, 8, 9, 10};

        // Parallel stream to compute sum
        int sum = Arrays.stream(numbers)
                        .parallel()
                        .sum();
```

```
        System.out.println("Sum: " + sum);
    }
}
```

Explanation:

The `Arrays.stream(numbers).parallel()` converts the stream into a parallel stream, allowing operations like `sum()` to be performed concurrently across multiple CPU cores.

Java's Memory Model and Atomic Operations

Java's **Memory Model (JMM)** defines how threads interact with memory and how variables are shared between them. It ensures that multi-threaded programs are consistent and predictable by specifying **visibility** and **ordering** of variables between threads.

Key Concepts of JMM:

Visibility: Changes made by one thread to shared variables may not be visible to other threads immediately.

Ordering: The order in which operations are executed in one thread might not match the order in which they appear in the source code.

Atomic Operations and the `java.util.concurrent` Package

Java provides atomic operations for safe interaction with shared variables across threads. The **Atomic** classes in the `java.util.concurrent.atomic` package (like AtomicInteger, AtomicLong, AtomicReference) ensure that operations like incrementing a value or comparing and updating a value are done atomically.

Example: Using AtomicInteger

```java
java

import java.util.concurrent.atomic.AtomicInteger;

public class AtomicExample {
    public static void main(String[] args) {
        AtomicInteger count = new AtomicInteger(0);

        // Atomic increment
        count.incrementAndGet();
        System.out.println("Count after increment: " + count.get());

        // Atomic compare and set
        boolean updated = count.compareAndSet(1, 2);
```

```
        System.out.println("Compare    and    set
successful: " + updated);
        System.out.println("Updated    count:    "    +
count.get());
    }
}
```

Explanation:

`AtomicInteger` ensures thread-safe operations when incrementing the counter.

`incrementAndGet()` atomically increments the value.

`compareAndSet()` compares the current value and, if it matches the expected value, updates it atomically.

Real-World Example: Optimizing a High-Performance Trading Application for Low-Latency Execution

In a **high-frequency trading application**, minimizing latency and maximizing throughput are paramount. Java's **JVM tuning**, **advanced concurrency**, and **atomic operations** can be leveraged to optimize such applications.

Optimizing the JVM for Low-Latency Trading

Heap Management: Use **G1 Garbage Collection** for low-latency requirements.

Thread Management: Use a **FixedThreadPool** to manage threads efficiently and avoid thread creation overhead.

Atomic Operations: Use `AtomicInteger` to manage counters and trade quantities without locking.

JVM Tuning Example for Low Latency:
bash

```
java    -Xms2g    -Xmx2g    -XX:+UseG1GC    -
XX:MaxGCPauseMillis=10 -XX:ParallelGCThreads=8 -
XX:+UnlockDiagnosticVMOptions                -
XX:+PrintGCDetails        -XX:+PrintGCDateStamps
TradingApp
```

Explanation:

G1 GC minimizes garbage collection pauses.

MaxGCPauseMillis ensures garbage collection pauses are kept below 10 ms.

ParallelGCThreads utilizes multiple threads for garbage collection to minimize its impact on performance.

357

Conclusion

In this chapter, we:

- Explored **JVM tuning and performance optimization** techniques, including garbage collection and heap management.

- Covered **advanced concurrency** techniques using the **ExecutorService, Fork/Join**, and **parallel streams** for building efficient, multi-threaded applications.

- Examined **Java's memory model** and how **atomic operations** ensure thread safety in concurrent applications.

- Demonstrated how these techniques can be applied in a **high-performance trading application** to achieve low-latency execution and optimal performance.

Java offers powerful tools and techniques for optimizing performance, especially in applications that require high concurrency and minimal latency. In the next chapter, we will delve into **Java's modular system** introduced in Java 9, which helps manage large codebases and modularize applications effectively. Let's continue enhancing our Java expertise!

CHAPTER 27

BEST PRACTICES AND FINAL THOUGHTS

In this final chapter, we will reflect on some of the most important **best practices** for writing **clean** and **maintainable code** in Java. We will also discuss **Java coding standards**, how to ensure that your code remains readable and efficient, and how to **continuously improve** as a Java developer. Finally, we will walk through a **real-world example** of refactoring a legacy Java application to adhere to modern coding standards, demonstrating how to apply these practices effectively in your own projects.

Writing Clean, Maintainable Code in Java

Writing **clean** and **maintainable** code is crucial for the long-term success of software projects. Clean code is easy to read, understand, and modify. It reduces the likelihood of bugs and technical debt while improving the overall efficiency of development.

Key Principles of Clean Code

Readability: Code should be easy to read and understand. Clear names for variables, methods, and classes are crucial.

Consistency: Follow consistent naming conventions, formatting, and styles throughout the project.

Simplicity: Avoid over-complicating solutions. Favor simple solutions that solve the problem effectively.

Separation of Concerns: Keep different responsibilities in different classes, methods, and modules.

Avoid Duplication: Reuse code and avoid repeating the same logic. **DRY (Don't Repeat Yourself)** principle is key.

Write Tests: Write unit tests to verify that your code works as expected and to ensure that future changes don't introduce bugs.

Commenting: Comment **why** something is done, not **what** is done. The code itself should convey the "what" clearly.

Refactoring: Continuously improve your code by refactoring it to simplify and optimize without changing its behavior.

Example: Writing Clean and Maintainable Code

Consider this simple class that calculates the area of different shapes. We will make sure it follows clean code principles:

```java
public class ShapeAreaCalculator {

    public double calculateArea(String
shapeType, double... dimensions) {
        if (shapeType == null || dimensions ==
null || dimensions.length == 0) {
            throw                          new
IllegalArgumentException("Shape     type    and
dimensions must be provided");
        }

        switch (shapeType.toLowerCase()) {
            case "circle":
                return
calculateCircleArea(dimensions[0]);
            case "rectangle":
                return
calculateRectangleArea(dimensions[0],
dimensions[1]);
            case "triangle":
```

```
            return
calculateTriangleArea(dimensions[0],
dimensions[1]);
            default:
                throw                    new
IllegalArgumentException("Unsupported    shape
type: " + shapeType);
        }
    }


    private   double   calculateCircleArea(double
radius) {
        return Math.PI * radius * radius;
    }


    private double calculateRectangleArea(double
length, double width) {
        return length * width;
    }


    private  double  calculateTriangleArea(double
base, double height) {
        return 0.5 * base * height;
    }
}
```

Explanation:

The code is **modular** and each method has a **single responsibility**.

362

The method names and class are descriptive, making the code **self-documenting**.

The **switch-case** structure makes it easy to add more shape types in the future.

Java Coding Standards and Best Practices

Following **Java coding standards** ensures that code remains consistent, readable, and maintainable, especially in large teams or open-source projects.

Java Coding Standards

Naming Conventions:

Classes: Use **PascalCase** (e.g., `ShapeAreaCalculator`).

Methods: Use **camelCase** (e.g., `calculateArea`).

Variables: Use **camelCase** (e.g., `circleArea`).

Constants: Use **UPPER_CASE_WITH_UNDERSCORES** (e.g., `MAX_SIZE`).

Indentation and Formatting:

Use **4 spaces** for indentation, not tabs.

Keep lines of code **under 80 characters** to improve readability.

Use **blank lines** to separate logical blocks of code.

Braces:

Always use braces ({ }) for control statements, even for single-line statements.

```java

if (condition) {
    // Do something
}
```

Documentation:

Use **JavaDoc** for documenting public classes and methods.

Include a **description** of the class, method parameters, and return values.

```java

/**
 * Calculates the area of a circle.
```

```
    *
    * @param radius the radius of the circle
    * @return the area of the circle
    */
public double calculateCircleArea(double
radius) {
    return Math.PI * radius * radius;
}
```

Avoid Hardcoding:

Avoid hardcoding values such as file paths, numbers, or strings. Use **constants** or configuration files.

How to Continue Learning and Growing as a Java Developer

Java is a vast ecosystem with continuous evolution. As a Java developer, it is important to **stay up to date** with the latest features, tools, and best practices. Here are some ways you can continue learning and growing:

Practice Regularly:

Build real-world projects to apply your learning.

Contribute to open-source projects to gain exposure to large codebases and collaboration.

Follow the Java Community:

Join Java-related forums, mailing lists, and communities such as **Stack Overflow**, **Java Reddit**, and **DZone**.

Attend Java conferences and meetups to network with other professionals and learn from experts.

Read Books and Articles:

Some great books for Java developers include:

Effective Java by Joshua Bloch

Java Concurrency in Practice by Brian Goetz

Spring in Action by Craig Walls

Learn New Technologies:

Explore modern Java frameworks like **Spring Boot**, **Quarkus**, and **Micronaut**.

Dive into **microservices, containers (Docker)**, and **cloud technologies (AWS, GCP, Azure)**.

Understand **DevOps practices** and tools like **Jenkins**, **Maven**, and **Gradle**.

Improve Your Soft Skills:

Enhance your problem-solving and algorithmic thinking by practicing on platforms like **LeetCode**, **HackerRank**, and **Codewars**.

Work on **communication skills**, as explaining technical concepts is key to working in teams.

Real-World Example: Refactoring a Legacy Java Application for Modern Standards

Let's walk through a **real-world example** of refactoring a legacy Java application to adhere to modern standards.

Legacy Application: A Simple Email Notification System

Imagine a legacy email notification system written in Java, which has the following problems:

Hardcoded values (e.g., SMTP server address).

Poor naming conventions.

Lack of modularity.

Legacy Code:

java

```java
public class EmailNotifier {
    public void sendNotification(String to,
String message) {
        String smtpServer =
"smtp.legacyserver.com";
        // Connect to SMTP server
        // Send email
    }
}
```

Refactoring for Modern Standards

We will refactor the legacy code to:

Use configuration properties for SMTP server addresses.

Apply meaningful variable names.

Modularize the code using proper separation of concerns.

Use Java 8 features where appropriate.

Refactored Code:

java

```java
import java.util.Properties;
```

```java
import javax.mail.*;
import javax.mail.internet.*;

public class EmailNotifier {
    private String smtpServer;
    private String fromAddress;

    // Constructor initializes values from configuration
    public EmailNotifier(String smtpServer, String fromAddress) {
        this.smtpServer = smtpServer;
        this.fromAddress = fromAddress;
    }

    public void sendNotification(String to, String subject, String message) {
        Properties properties = System.getProperties();
        properties.put("mail.smtp.host", smtpServer);

        Session session = Session.getDefaultInstance(properties);

        try {
            MimeMessage mimeMessage = new MimeMessage(session);
```

```
        mimeMessage.setFrom(new
InternetAddress(fromAddress));

mimeMessage.addRecipient(Message.RecipientType.
TO, new InternetAddress(to));
        mimeMessage.setSubject(subject);
        mimeMessage.setText(message);
        Transport.send(mimeMessage);
    } catch (MessagingException e) {
        e.printStackTrace();
    }
  }
}
```

Explanation:

We replaced the hardcoded SMTP server address with a configurable one passed into the constructor.

Used **meaningful variable names** like smtpServer and fromAddress.

We now handle the Session and email sending in a modular and flexible way.

This refactor improves readability, flexibility, and maintainability.

Conclusion

In this final chapter, we:

Learned how to write **clean, maintainable code** by following **best practices** and **Java coding standards**.

Discussed ways to **continuously improve** as a Java developer through practice, community involvement, and continuous learning.

Refactored a **legacy Java application** to modern standards, demonstrating the importance of adhering to modern coding practices.

By following these principles and consistently improving your skills, you will become a better Java developer and be able to build more scalable, efficient, and maintainable applications. Java is a powerful language with a rich ecosystem, and your journey to mastering it is a continuous process. Keep learning, keep coding, and enjoy the process of building great software!

www.ingramcontent.com/pod-product-compliance
Lightning Source LLC
La Vergne TN
LVHW051427050326
832903LV00030BD/2953